MOMENTS OF THE ROSE

MOMENTS OF THE ROSE

A TAPESTRY OF NORTHAMPTONSHIRE
TALES

IAN ADDIS

Illustrated by
Robert Mercer

for Jean
best wishes
Ian Addis

JEMA PUBLICATIONS

Pat and Stephanie, for their patience.

IAN ADDIS

Ian Addis is headteacher at Barton Seagrave Primary School. Married with two grown up children he lives in Kettering, the town where he was born and raised. He was educated at Kettering Grammar School and the College of St Mark and St John in Chelsea before beginning a teaching career in 1963. After working in several local schools he obtained a headship at Geddington in 1977 where he served for ten years before assuming his present post.

A first book, "What Can The Matter Be", a collection of children's stories published in 1992 shortly after his fiftieth birthday was quickly followed by a compilation of material for use in School Assembly. ("Assemblies", Scholastic Publications, March 1994).

A passionate football devotee and ex-player he much admires author Nick Hornby's "Fever Pitch", a book he would dearly loved to have written himself.

ROBERT MERCER

Robert Mercer also lives in Kettering and prior to retirement was employed for many years as a headteacher by Northamptonshire County Council. Despite the demands of his career he has always tried to ensure that painting materials remained close at hand. For much of that time he was involved in a wide variety of 'art teaching' situations as diverse as A Level students, Borstal boys and Senior Citizens, and has run art classes for Northampton Adult Education Service continuously for over twenty years.

Deeply committed to his own painting he has included work in many mixed exhibitions and held several one man shows to date. Having always enjoyed the discipline and delight of pure drawing his task in illustrating Ian's fascinating book proved to be a very enjoyable one.

ACKNOWLEDGEMENTS

Perhaps the most rewarding aspect of the entire project was the amount of encouragement and support received from individuals and organisations named below. Many gave so generously of time, afforded warm hospitality and unselfishly shared the fruit of their own research to assist in the compilation of this book. The list may well be incomplete however, and I apologise for any inadvertent omission.

J L Carr, Colin Eaton and the staff of Northampton Central Library, Jerome Betts, Joyce and Maurice Palmer, Peter Eads, Dick Hackney, Ian Mayes, the staff at Kettering Public Library, the County Record Office, Northampton Mercury, Kettering Evening Telegraph, Stamford Mercury, Valerie Panther, Stephen Exley, The Kettering Bookshop, Tony Ireson, Ron Wilson, Ron Sismey, Tony Smith, Beryl Carrington, Byron Rogers, Trevor Hold, Gerald Walker, and Tony Noble without whose enthusiasm the project would never have materialised.

Ian Addis

NORTHAMPTONSHIRE

- location of the stories

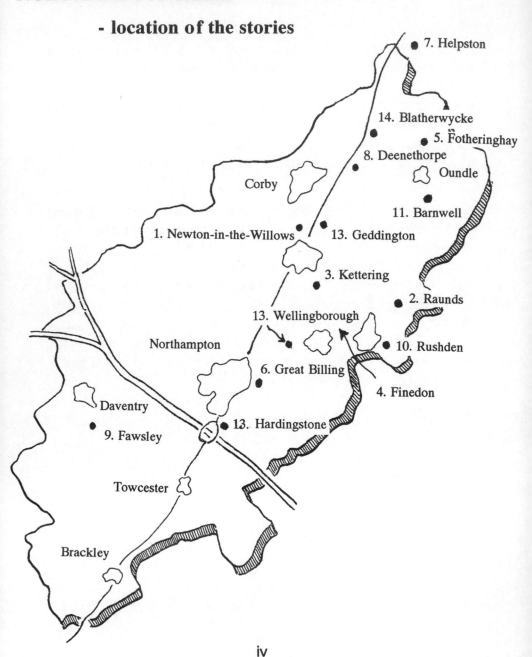

7. Helpston

14. Blatherwycke

5. Fotheringhay

8. Deenethorpe

Corby

Oundle

11. Barnwell

1. Newton-in-the-Willows

13. Geddington

3. Kettering

2. Raunds

13. Wellingborough

10. Rushden

Northampton

6. Great Billing

4. Finedon

Daventry

13. Hardingstone

9. Fawsley

Towcester

Brackley

CONTENTS

INTRODUCTION

My grandparents lived on Rose Hill in Finedon and every Sunday afternoon when I was little we went to visit.

Between ritual inspections of family graves in the shadow of the doomed Volta Tower and the inevitable ham salad teas, I usually managed to escape upstairs to the spare bedroom.

Undisturbed I would pore over drawers full of old photographs, suck on grandad's collection of briar pipes and ponder curious words embroidered on a sampler which hung over the redundant fireplace.

"If thou of fortune be bereft

And of thine earthly store

hath left

Two loaves, sell one, and with

the dole

Buy hyacinths to feed the soul."

Certainly far beyond the comprehension of an eight year old, yet the words were consigned to memory, that great depository where jumbled baggage from our past lies randomly gathering dust.

Remarkably however, years later, we can often locate and unearth the very piece to match the moment. So it was with Captain Pouch.

Last April, when invited to contribute to a collection of history stories for children, I sought a Northamptonshire character both wholly authentic and rich in appeal. After much cogitation I recalled a conversation some years earlier with novelist and historian J L Carr. He had given a characteristically colourful account of events leading to an ancient battle in the fields around the village of Newton and the ensuing defeat of the mysterious Captain's army.

There was my story. But how often had I visited the Field Study Centre at St Faith's Church unaware of its tragic connection with that remarkable early champion of human rights. I resolved to pursue other shadows from the past following the increasingly complex trail into overgrown grave-yards, through tangled undergrowth, sodden corn fields and sprawling housing estates, dragging along artist colleague Robert Mercer, whose rich contributions to this book are not confined to his evocative illustrations.

So much emerged, fact vied with fancy, and as in tapestry the threads intriguingly wove themselves together, linking people and places across the centuries.

It may well be that these tales can do scant justice to all the richness they depict. Yet perhaps the fleeting fragrances will lead the inquisitive reader to explore still further into the rose garden.

Ian Addis

Kettering

January 1994

1

THE STORY OF CAPTAIN POUCH

The army of giant diggers worked swiftly, uprooting hedgerows, smashing fences, filling ditches.

Within hours the patchwork of tiny fields was transformed into a vast prairie, awaiting the plough, the seed drill and combine harvester. What John Reynolds would have given for a J.C.B. or two instead of an axe, a spade and a certainty that right was on his side.

But that was almost four hundred years ago. In 1607 to be precise.

Hard up King James I had hit upon a novel idea for raising money to replenish his dwindling royal purse. He sold off Crown property, including acres of Royal Forest, to local landowners who clamoured to buy.

Squire Tresham purchased woodland around the village of Newton-in-the-Willows in Northamptonshire and proceeded to fell valuable timber, clear the ground and enclose the land as pasture for sheep. There was money in wool.

But he soon discovered problems lurking in the undergrowth. For centuries peasants had settled in the forests and on wasteland, building houses, raising families, cultivating the soil and making use of the plentiful fuel. They weren't vagrants or vagabonds but law abiding people, who over the years had come to regard this common land as their own.

Now they were confronted with hedges and fences where none had stood within memory, found roads and paths blocked as Tresham's estate grew and were turned out of their houses at the stroke of a lawyer's pen. Not surprisingly they didn't take kindly to the Squire's plans.

Faced with a choice either to abandon their homes and livelihoods and move away destitute, or to destroy the hedges and fences and stay put, they chose the latter.

They called themselves "levellers" and rallied around their chosen leader. That man was John Reynolds.

Not a very heroic name was it? Hardly a Sir Francis Drake or Sir Walter Raleigh. John Reynolds didn't think so either. That's why he called himself Captain Pouch.

It was a strange but clever choice of name.

".... Her charitable tongue,

Like the old rebels of Northamptonshire,

Cannot endure hedges of teeth should stand

To make her mouth enclosure."

Thomas Randolph "Hey for Honesty, Down with Knavery" London 1651

His followers had adopted the cause with good reason. Many were filled with a sense of injustice at being hustled from their homes and land. Others hated the landowners and welcomed a chance to get even. There was widespread support, even from the clergy. Parsons preached in local churches of the suffering and hardship brought by enclosure upon displaced families, who were rather like modern day refugees. But this was also an age of superstition.

Reynolds announced that the great leather pouch hanging from his belt contained "sufficient matter to defend against all comers". In other words he claimed to possess a magic charm that would protect everyone who followed him, provided they "refrained from evil deeds".

He also affected authority from both God and the King to "throw down enclosures".

All around the district as fast as fences were put up the levellers tore them down. But matters quickly came to a head when reports of rebellion reached London and the King.

A Royal Proclamation of May 30th 1607 instructed the Lord Lieutenant of the County, Sir Robert Cecil, and his deputies to "immediately suppress (the levellers) by whatever means they may, be it force of arms if other lawful means do not serve and reduce them to their duties."

It was the practice in such circumstances to call up the Trained Bands, a kind of Home Guard led by the local gentry, which each parish had to arm. In this instance, however, such a force could prove unreliable. Would they attack their own neighbours? Many sympathised with the levellers while others were actually related to members of Pouch's 'army'.

In the event the Lieutenants mobilised every reliable servant that local gentlemen could arm.

"....the great leather pouch hanging from his belt contained sufficient matter to defend against all corners."

On the morning of June 8th, the two groups faced each other across the valley of the River Ise below Newton village. On one side, according to eye witnesses, as many as a thousand men and women, armed with half pikes, staves, bows, axes and stones. On the other, footmen with muskets and calivers.

Magistrates read a Royal Proclamation ordering the crowd to disperse.

No-one moved.

The order was repeated.

Perhaps an odd one or two slipped away.

Then the attack began.

A volley of shots was fired into the massed ranks.

Then charging horsemen drove deep into the crowd, scattering the levellers in all directions. They quickly regrouped but a second charge ended the battle. Captain Pouch's army was defeated.

Later the Earl of Shrewsbury wrote "The first charge they stood and fought desperately: But at the second charge they ran away in which were slain some forty or fifty of them and a great number hurt".

The dead and dying were carried to St Faith's church nearby. Punishment was swift and severe. Ringleaders were tried and executed, and their remains displayed around the County as a warning to others. Whether Captain Pouch died in the fight or was hanged after it is not certain. No records of the Assize Rolls or those killed in battle survive. But it is said that afterwards his famous pouch was opened and was found to contain .... a few crumbs of green cheese.

What of the levellers who fought and Lived?

The names of 143 are recorded in a document still extant,

wherein they were required to sign a declaration promising to behave themselves for the rest of their lives:

"We and everyone of us whose names are here underwritten .... do most humbly acknowledge our heinous offence .... in the late rebellion .... upon pretence of depopulation and unlawful Inclosure and are most heartily sorry for the same. We acknowledge with all thankfulness his Majesty's gracious and exceeding clemency in setting wide open to us the gate of his mercy ...."

Occupations are listed too. They include butchers, bakers, labourers, shepherds, carpenters, coopers....... Ancestors of local people almost certainly unaware of their rebellious forebears.

Today, Squire Tresham's hedges and fences around Newton are levelled by machines as pasture once more gives way to the plough. But stand quietly in the shelter of St Faith's church, and close your eyes.

Listen.

That distant murmur might be the diggers, or traffic on the new motorway far across the valley. Or it might even be the ghosts of Captain Pouch's army massing in the fields below.

2

THE MAN IN THE RED TIE

Which general led an army 115 strong, on a route march 70 miles long to do battle with the Secretary of State for War himself?

The answer, James Gribble, begs even more questions.

It's a fascinating story.

There has been a centuries old tradition of boot and shoe making in Northamptonshire, due in part to the abundance of good grazing land for cattle and the profusion of oak forests providing bark for tanning. The industry had its humble origins in barns and sheds at the bottom of gardens, where whole families were engaged in the manufacture of the complete boot or shoe. By the 1850's it had developed into a primitive factory system like William Nichols' Grove Street establishment in Raunds. Here the clickers, (men who cut the leather according to patterns), were kept on the premises, but the closing, (hand sewing of the uppers), and making, (attaching the soles and heels), were put to outworkers. At this time shoeworkers prided their independence and were to some extent a law unto themselves. In his autobiography "The Vanished World", H E Bates describes their inclination to "... get rousing drunk on Saturdays and Sundays, never by tradition working on Mondays. Either out of duty to their patron saint St Crispin or in pursuit of a cure for mountainous hangovers, they sought solace in the surrounding countryside ......"

Such anarchic behaviour had no place in the regulated factory regimes which were becoming more widespread amongst the shoeworking communities. As the manufacturers began to enforce strict rules governing working hours, attendance and rates of pay, workers realised the need to protect their own interests. A first Trade union, the Amalgamated Cordwainers Association, became the National Union of Boot and Shoe Riveters and Finishers in 1874, and in turn the National Union of Boot and Shoe Operatives sixteen years later.

The industry was entering a critical period.

The Boer War had stimulated the need for army boots and for its duration, ensured relative prosperity for workers in the principal county centres of Raunds, Finedon, Irthlingborough, Higham Ferrers, Rushden, Wellingborough and Kettering. The end of hostilities however brought a slump with the immediate fall in demand. Factories began undercutting each other to get contracts and such contracts as were available were less lucrative than before. Not only was the rate paid to a skilled, proficient bootmaker reduced from a wartime peak of 3/11d (20p) per pair to 2/6d (12p) by 1905, but improved standards were imposed following claims that poor quality boots had been issued during the conflict.

Living standards fell as, "the average (worker) can do only six pairs in a 54 hour week."

Unemployment and short time working became commonplace. The small town of Raunds was particularly hard hit by the recession as during the war it had become the centre of Government contract work with a dozen boot factories employing over 1200 workers.

In the autumn of 1904 the Secretary of State for War, Mr Forster, was petitioned to implement a "fair wages" clause in Government contracts in a bid to restore wage levels. He refused, but urged the men to use the power of their union to argue the case directly with manufacturers. The response of the National Union of Boot and Shoe Operatives was immediate and dramatic. Enter a short, stocky man wearing his habitual red tie.

James Gribble.

He was born at 25 Bailiff Street, Northampton in January 1868 the eldest child of a family of nine. His father, also James, worked in the shoe trade but was once landlord of the "Marquis of Carabas" public house in Bouverie Street. Young James had only a rudimentary formal education at Spring Lane and Vernon Terrace Board Schools, before briefly attending the Northampton Evening School in his teens, for at the age of 12 he had begun work for boot manufacturers Turner Brothers, Hyde and Co. Five years later in 1885 and unemployed, he enlisted in the regular army serving for eighteen months in England before moving overseas. He attained the rank of acting quarter master sergeant before demobilisation in January 1893.

On his return to civilian life and work in the boot trade, Gribble quickly became immersed in local union affairs. Despite a justifiable reputation for hotheaded unruly behaviour, which probably destroyed his chances of achieving high office in the Socialist movement, by Autumn 1904 he had been appointed National Union organiser and was sent to Raunds to stimulate activity at which point he takes centre stage in our story.

On March 11th 1905, having failed to achieve agreement with any local manufacturers to accept the uniform wage rates endorsed by the War Office, the Raunds bootmakers went on strike.

In a speech typically radical and antagonistic towards these recalcitrant employers, Gribble described the town as, "..... a few compounds dumped there, surrounded by houses inhabited by white slaves, who ground out profits for the owners of the compound ...."

Although some manufacturers succumbed to Gribble's robust negotiating abilities, the hard core majority resisted. The strike dragged on into April leading to ugly scenes as the frustration of the workers spilled into violence, much of it directed towards the employers and strike breakers. The media had a field day.

Newspapers carried reports of riots, serious disturbances and extensive damage. The Manchester Guardian attempted to redress the balance reducing the "riots" to "accidental outbursts of horseplay", "extensive damage" to "window smashing" and dismissing the possibility of "calling in the military" as "irresponsible nonsense."

With increasingly bad publicity generated by these disturbances, negotiations deadlocked, and a drift back to work by demoralised strikers, Gribble realised a dramatic gesture was required to regain public support. He decided to organise a march to London to put the strikers' case in person at the War

Office. If the deputation was refused an audience it would march on to see King Edward VII at Windsor Castle.

There was no shortage of volunteers. Eventually 115 representative strikers were selected by "General" Gribble who used his service experience to good effect. He was determined that the marchers would conduct themselves with dignity and discipline. The venture was planned with military precision. A Paymaster, Billetmaster and Commissariate-General were appointed as officers. Five companies were formed each with their own sergeants. The chosen men were drilled to perfection on a piece of wasteland near the Woodbine Club.

Monday, May 8th dawned clear and bright and the marchers set off from Raunds reaching Bedford that night.

Eleven bandsmen amongst the strikers borrowed instruments thus providing jaunty tunes to lead the marchers and raise the spirits. A corps of three cyclists rode ahead of the whole contingent. One unofficial marcher, Jack Pearson of Ringstead, went the whole distance on crutches!

After a public meeting on the Market Square at Bedford, accommodation was found in local homes, hotels and public buildings. The pattern was continued at Luton, St Albans and Watford before London was reached on Friday, May 12th.

Not one report in contemporary newspapers mentions hostility towards the marchers and everywhere contributions flooded into their strike collection fund. Ten thousand people gathered at Marble Arch to watch them arrive in the West End. Yet War Office officials at the Houses of Parliament refused to meet the deputation. Gribble, as ever resplendent in red tie, watched proceedings from the Strangers' Gallery becoming more and more annoyed by the likelihood that the strikers' case would never be heard. Characteristically his frustration boiled over.

He finally leapt to his feet and shouted, "Mr Speaker, is this gentleman trying to talk out time? For I've come here with 115 men from Northamptonshire who have marched all that way to lay their grievance before Mr Forster"

He was forcibly ejected. But not before it had been announced that an enquiry would be held in order to investigate wage levels in the army boot sector of the industry.

On Saturday evening James Gribble was part of an invited theatre audience who gathered to watch cinematographic film of the march. After the show, pride of place was reserved for Jack Pearson who demonstrated his expertise on crutches by bounding several times across the stage to rapturous applause.

The following afternoon "The General" addressed a vast crowd in Trafalgar Square sharing the platform with numerous eminent speakers including Suffragette Leader, Mrs Despard and Keir Hardie, the founder of the Labour Party.

The return march was completed on Saturday, May 20th when Gribble was carried shoulder high into the Woodbine Club by an excited crowd. He had certainly put the little Northampton-shire town on the map. The War Office enquiry supported the strikers demands and a Board of Conciliation and Arbitration was set up to deal with future difficulties. Raund's position as a leading producer of Army and Navy boots was assured for years to come.

Although committed to the need to politically educate working people James Gribble never achieved his ambition to repre sent Northampton as a Social Democrat (then an extreme left wing socialist party), Member of Parliament, failing to be elected in both 1906 and 1910.

Ill health forced his gradual withdrawal from public life and in

"The General addressed a vast crowd in Trafalgar Square."

1925 he retired to Hastings to take over the licence of a hotel there. Two years later he returned to Northampton, where he assisted in his wife's millinery business for several years. He died of a cerebral haemorrhage in Northampton General Hospital on August 14th 1934, aged 66 years old.

Perhaps it is as well that he didn't live to witness the postwar decline in Northamptonshire's boot and shoe trade and the demise of the work force that he, "General" Gribble had fought so hard to protect.

3

NOT JUST A PARK BUT A MAN

It had been a long journey. At the bottom of Barton Hill on the southern approach to Kettering, where the road turns sharply to the right and crosses a stone bridge over the River Ise, the young man stopped his steam ploughs and began to refill their boilers with water from the stream.

Suddenly the occupier of Barton Seagrave Hall appeared.

"Move those smoke belching monsters off the bridge," he ordered, "and leave that water alone!" Chastened the plough-man did as he was told. It was not an auspicious welcome to Kettering for one of its most famous names.

Charles Wicksteed was born in Leeds on the 30th March 1847.

His father was a minister who found the burden of working amongst the poor and needy in a busy industrial town intolerable. On doctor's advice he removed his family to "go and live like a cow," on a small holding in North Wales.

After two years, restored to good health by country living, he bought his own farm - Hafod-y-Coed - (Summer Abode in the Wood) near St Asaph.

Young Charles loved life on the farm. He watched with his father as the heavy clay soil was drained, learned to plough and care for the animals. To his father they were "livestock", to him they were friends. It was only in the matter of book learning that he was slow. So much so that he was not allowed to follow his brothers to grammar school but was sent away to board at a school in Lancaster. Although he was happy there

'Move those smoke belching monsters off the bridge"

he missed his parents, his eight brothers and sisters, his animals, and that freedom he enjoyed at the farm.

He left school at the age of 15 with no qualifications save a willingness to work hard and a determination to succeed.

At six o'clock on the morning of 3rd of March 1863 he entered the Leeds works of Messrs Kitson and Newetson to begin an engineering apprenticeship. Here he gained all the requirements of his trade, working in the machine shop, drawing office and with his great love, the locomotives. A job for life was guaranteed.

But Charles Wicksteed had bigger ideas. As an apprentice he had no real income and longed for the independence of running his own business. The opportunity came when some friends of his parents lent him the capital to purchase a couple of steam ploughs from a neighbouring factory.

So, at the age of 21, he set off with his own machines and his own team of workers to find employment on the rich farmlands of Norfolk. But, as he soon discovered, there was no fortune to be made. The summer of 1868 was one of the driest on record. There were constant problems. The land became so hard it bent the tynes of the cultivators and put excessive strain on the engines.

One evening, at dusk, whilst helping with the backing of a machine he became trapped between the plough and a cornstack. Hearing a cry, the driver cut off the steam, causing the engine to roll back into a furrow and onto the stack, crushing the young foreman. Jogged in a dogcart for seven miles to the hotel at Swaffham where he lodged, Charles was then carried awkwardly up stairs and along corridors, lain in a feather bed before being unskilfully attended by a local doctor. His broken leg was badly set an inch and a half shorter than the other causing him to limp for the rest of his life.

Nevertheless the work went on.

After three years ploughing on the sandy lands of the Norfolk estates he decided to move his engines onto the heavier soil of the Midlands. He headed westward towards Northampton for the summer. In July 1871 he wrote home from "The Van, near Kettering," describing his journey which had not been without dramatic incident.

Passing through a village on the outskirts of the town, sparks from the chimney of one engine set fire to a thatched roof. Luckily the flames were contained, but it cost £10 to repair the damage which was money he could hardly afford. And then of course there was the incident on the bridge.

Arriving in Kettering virtually penniless and still struggling to repay debts, Charles' ambition was as keen as ever. After much persuasion he succeeded in borrowing more money, this time from brother Hartley, and with it he began to build the Stamford Road Works.

It consisted simply of a room 40' x 20', a small engine, a ten inch lathe, a drilling machine for the purpose of repairing damaged ploughs, and the necessary benches. But this workshop, besides giving Charles a simple living, soon provided scope for his real talent - invention.

New tools were designed and marketed. Gradually his profits and good fortune began to grow. He found a house in Silver Street at a yearly rent of £19.00, married a local girl, Mary Gibb on December 13th 1877 and became a Liberal Councillor.

This gave him a platform for his controversial views on land ownership - "Not a square inch of this earth was made by man so no man had the right to call himself its owner"; social injustice and cruelty to animals, particularly vivisection. One of his early achievements was to promote the Rockingham Road

18

Park in the north end of town - a foretaste of things to come.

Lord Channing writes this description of him in 1894 "Charles Wicksteed with his strong features, often knitted brow, eyes burning with indignation or injustice, now lit up with open hearted generosity........"

By 1896, his machine tool business was prospering sufficiently for him to move into a new home large enough to accommodate his own growing family and his recently widowed mother.

Named "Bryn Hafod" (Hill summer abode), it was more than a building. Its gardens contained a summer house, fine trees, lawns and ponds and were open, not only to friends and relatives, but on Sundays to the general public.

"Closely bound to a human heart

Little brown dog, you had your part

In the levelling, building, staying of streams

In the park that arose from your master's dreams."

Hilda Wicksteed 1930

The fateful year of 1914 had far reaching consequences for Charles Wicksteed.In February Mary, his beloved wife and constant support and inspiration died. He completed the purchase of a small plantation, arable fields, a huge area of grassland and ironically that same winding stream where 43 years earlier he had stopped to water his steam ploughs.

In 1921 his dream of providing the people of Kettering with a "place of recreation, an object in their walks and a safe and happy playground for their children" was realised. With his constant companion Jerry, commemorated in stone as "the sweetest little dog in the world", he wandered its vast expanse planning the basic design. Its lake and wonderful collection of swings and slides equipped from his own factory, free to all. A miniature railway, golf course, restaurant and other amusements were added later.

Wicksteed's talent for invention was still very much alive. In "Kettering Revisited", Tony Smith informs that "In 1928 he designed a unique machine that could both slice and butter bread at a rate of two thousand slices an hour to feed hungry visitors".

On his death in March 1931 hundreds queued to pay their respects. As the coffin lay in state in the Park pavilion Jerry's lead was draped across its lid. Mourning their loss they were reminded of the great man's sadness some years before when his terrier had gone missing. Despite a widespread search and the offer of a generous reward the dog was never found.

But Charles Wicksteed never intended his park to be a place of grief. Today on sunny summer afternoons crowds still stream past the sign and in through the great iron gates to Wicksteed's.

Not just a park, but a man.

4

ROUGH JUSTICE?

Butch Cassidy and the Sundance Kid, Bonnie and Clyde, Ronald Biggs and the Great Train Robbers. Such infamous criminal partnerships are well known. Yet on the 9th April, 1813 Huffham White, Robert Kendall and Mary Howes were brought to trial at Northampton Assizes for a crime that was no less remarkable or audacious than any perpetrated by those more notorious villains.

The Leeds mail coach had stopped at Kettering during the early evening of October 12th 1812 to collect several sealed bags of letters from postmistress Mrs Stockburn.

Guard John Gardner put them in the mailbox under his seat, locked it by snapping the padlock and assumed his position at the back. The coach, carrying four inside passengers, then resumed its journey to London at about a quarter to six. The box was next checked at Burton Latimer when a bag of local mail was dropped off. All was intact. After again snapping the lock and hearing it fasten, Gardner lit the lamps before taking his place at the back once more.

A short time later, while climbing the brow of Burton Hill towards Finedon, he clambered over the coach to sit alongside the coachman until they reached the outskirts of Higham Ferrers. He then returned to his seat, sounded the posthorn warning of their arrival and the coach pulled into the Green Dragon Inn at around 7 o'clock.

When he examined the mailbox once more he knew immediately it had been robbed. The lock had disappeared yet there was no indication that force had been used. All the mailbags except three had been taken. Somewhere between Burton and Higham, while Gardner sat with the coachman, the lock had been picked and the contents removed with no one any the wiser.

In the early hours of the following morning Thomas Warren, a Rushden man, was travelling to Harborough market. A short distance from the obelisk near Finedon crossroads he noticed an object lying in the road. It was too dark to examine it closely so he threw it on his cart and waited until he reached Rothwell where he found it to be a sack containing a number of empty bags. These he delivered to the magistrate at Higham on his return that evening.

It was three months later before more evidence was found. Travelling from Islip to Newport Pagnell, apprentice John Green found a sack in a spinney known as 'The Poplars' on the Thrapston Road again close to Finedon crossroads. The bags inside were empty but some were proven to have been part of a consignment from Barnsley dispatched on the Leeds mail. Everything now pointed to the robbery having taken place as the coach slowed on its journey up the steep hill through Finedon towards Irthlingborough.

Although he lived at Wellingborough, Robert Kendall often frequented the tollgate cottage at Keyston, near Bythorn, where Huffham White and Mary Howes had lived for about two years. Various witnesses testified that the two men had travelled to Wellingborough on the day of the robbery. The publican of the Woolpack Inn at Islip timed their arrival, in a two wheeled cart with "Kendall Keyston Bar" painted on the side, as a little after 4.00 p.m. They drank for nearly an hour and by five o'clock had reached the tollgate on the outskirts of the village where they conversed with the keeper. A labourer working in a field close to the Wellingborough road in Finedon around dusk, heard the mail coach go past. About half an hour later he saw two men, assumed to be Kendall and White, pass by in a gig or cart. Under oath he maintained that one said, "It is a complete job, damn you, drive on."

Other witnesses reported that a horse drawn cart passed through the tollbar on the outskirts of Finedon between seven and eight o'clock. After discussing who should pay the toll, one man climbed the footstile while the other drove the cart through the gate. The keeper alleged it to be the only vehicle to pass through all evening. Kendall and White were seen together in Wellingborough that night but the following morning White returned to Bythorn in a post chaise. Kendall explained

"The robbery took place as the coach slowed on its journey up the steep hill through Finedon."

the extravagance to a witness by describing White as "a man of property".

Later that week Kendall was arrested by a Bow Street Officer. He had made no attempt to leave the area, was apprehended at Wellingborough Fair and interrogated at the Hind Inn. When he was informed that he was suspected of complicity in the mail coach robbery he consented to a search of his house. Unbeknown to Kendall two fifty pound notes were discovered inside a pocket book kept in a drawer in the sitting room. As the officer had no information regarding the notes he was compelled to return the next day having instructed the suspect to remain at home overnight. The next day the notes had disappeared. On the strength of this "evidence", circumstantial as it appears, Kendall was arrested. In his statement he denied any involvement in the robbery or knowledge of the person who travelled with him in the cart to Wellingborough on the day of the crime.

White meantime had returned to Bythorn, collected Mary Howes and travelled to London by way of the York Mail coach. She was arrested in the capital a few days later and was committed to prison with Robert Kendall on November 5th. White eluded capture until the following Spring.

His arrest in Liverpool followed months of intensive police activity and detective work. A reward of £200 was offered by the Post Office for his apprehension and conviction and wanted posters displayed throughout the country. From these we can deduce that White, unlike Kendall, was undoubtedly a hardened and habitual criminal. Sentenced to transportation he had twice escaped from the prison hulks to commit further robberies.

Cheques, bills and notes from the Leeds Mail were soon circulating around the London criminal fraternity. The police followed White's trail from London to Bath to Bristol. There an undercover agent, disguised as a sailor, tracked him to a house in Ratcliff Meads. He again evaded capture but a search of the house revealed five pistols. Finally, on April 1st 1813, a Liverpool constable succeeded in overpowering White and a subsequent search of a house in Scotland Road unearthed a great number of pick locks, "every apparatus for opening locks and forcing doors", concealed under a flagstone in the cellar.

And so the trial began. It lasted for fourteen and a half hours. Mary Howes was acquitted of being an accessory but Kendall and White were found guilty of robbing the mail coach and, "under an Act of Parliament passed in the reign of His present Majesty", sentenced to death.

The executions took place on Friday, August 13th on Northampton Racecourse in front of a huge public gathering. They led to fierce debate and argument, particularly among clergy, as to the justice of Kendall's punishment. He had persistently denied carrying out the crime, describing as unfortunate the set of circumstances that fatally linked himself to White, and faced death with both piety and dignity.

At the place of execution he reasserted his innocence, declaring "he should be a murdered man in respect to the crime for which he was about to suffer."

It is interesting that White, who apparently displayed contempt to the end for all around him, supported Kendall's contention.

After the death sentence had been passed he addressed the

Judge so. "My Lord, I hope you will have mercy upon Kendall for he was not the man who robbed the coach."

Rough justice?

5

JUST A PILE OF STONES

"£100 are urgently required to preserve from further spoilation the remnant of the great castle so intimately connected with English and Scottish National History and Royalty since the period of the Norman Conquest."

Fortunately the response to this appeal by Peterborough Archaeological Society early this century was successful in providing a six foot iron railing to protect a pile of stones on a grassy slope above the River Nene. For these stones are the remains of Fotheringhay castle and few places in Britain hide such a rich or tragic past.

The castle was built in 1100 by Simon de Senlis, son in law of William the Conqueror's niece Judith and first Norman Earl of Northampton. The property passed by marriage to Malcolm and William, both Kings of Scotland, and successively to the Earl of Richmond, the Countess of Pembroke and eventually Edmund Plantagenant founder of the House of York. In 1460 his nephew Richard claimed the English throne following victory in the Battle of Northampton. Alas in the same year Richard was defeated at Wakefield, crowned with a "wreath of grass" before being executed along with his son Edmund. Nevertheless, dynastically all was not lost.

Two of his widow Cicely's fifteen children were indeed destined to be Kings. Edward IV and Richard III, the latter born at the castle. The badge of the House of York, a falcon and fetterlock, on the windvane above the nearby church provides a fitting memorial to the illustrious members of the family buried within.

But mention Fotheringhay and most people think of a Queen, and a Scottish one at that.

Mary, Catholic grandaughter of Henry VII, was crowned Queen of Scotland at the age of nine months on the 9th September 1543. Her life was a catalogue of sad events. Marriage at 15 to the French Dauphin ended two years later with her husband's death. During this absence in France her cousin Elizabeth had become England's Protestant Queen and Protestantism too had replaced Catholicism as Scotland's official religion.

On her return the beautiful auburn haired girl widow was courted by suitors from almost every Royal House in Europe. Foolishly she chose to marry Henry Stewart, Lord Darnley and soon bore his son, the heir to the Scottish throne. Darnley, however, had ambition to be king himself usurping Mary's rights. When this power was denied on the advice of Mary's private secretary Rizzio, Darnley authorised his murder. Discovering her husband's implication in the killing and feeling increasingly at risk herself Mary left Darnley. She quickly found solace with the Earl of Bothwell, another injudicious choice, who urged her to agree to a divorce. She consented provided that her son's right to succeed was not endangered. Darnley's mysterious death following a gunpowder explosion at the house where he was recuperating from illness added to the intrigue. How much Mary knew of the plot to kill her husband is uncertain. After a mock trial Bothwell was acquitted, divorced his own wife and married the Queen on 15th May 1567, only three months after Darnley's death.

Such dark intrigue and power broking proved too much for the Scottish Lords and a group of powerful nobles set off to arrest her new husband. Bothwell fled leaving Mary to make terms or follow him. Disguised as a pageboy she escaped to meet up with the Earl and their supporters in Dunbar. An army was then summoned to "rescue the queen". The two sides met but the short battle was one sided and Mary's forces quickly surrendered. Bothwell again fled, this time abroad, but the Queen, after brief imprisonment on the Isle of Loch Levan where she was forced to accept abdication, escaped to cross the border into England, there to throw herself on Elizabeth's mercy. Mary begged her cousin that she would not "be made the Sport of Fate." But that is what she became.

For the next twenty years she was under house arrest. It was in reality prison. Tutbury, Coventry, Sheffield, Wingfield Manor, gloomy Tutbury once more, Chartley and finally on September 25th 1584, she arrived at Fotheringhay Castle.

Meanwhile the outside world, particularly that of Catholic Europe was full of continuing conspiracy and intrigue, much of it linked to Mary. Imminent war with Spain, and the growing fear of invasion made her very existence a dangerous embarrassment to Elizabeth who was constantly urged by her advisers to remove the threat once and for all. It was the exposure of the Babbington plot to assassinate Elizabeth and free Mary that finally forced the English Queen's hand.

Despite little direct evidence as to her personal involvement Mary was charged with treason, perceived to be "an imaginer of Her Majesty's destruction."

After a long trial in which she conducted her own defence with courage and skill, where witnesses too ashamed to testify in her presence gave evidence by proxy, where vital information was known to have been obtained by torture, the judgement was referred to the Star Chamber which found her guilty in her absence. Elizabeth, conscious of Mary's powerful friends in Spain, signed the fateful warrant on February 1st 1587. Haste

"She descended the staircase into the great banqueting hall."

to carryout the sentence overtook any intention that Queen Elizabeth may have had to revoke the death penalty. Secrecy surrounded her advisers' plans. It is said that the death warrant was concealed in a pile of miscellaneous documents for signing by a prevaricating Queen.

Bull, the London hangman, was summoned. He agreed to behead Mary for a fee of £10, arriving in Fotheringhay disguised as a servant with his axe hidden in a trunk.

Mary spent the evening of February 7th tying up gifts for her servants in little purses and in writing letters of farewell. She slept some hours, then waking spent the rest of the night in prayer. According to historian H V Morton she received a consecrated wafer from the Pope with dispensation to administer the sacrament herself. This she did the next morning a few hours before descending the staircase into the great Banqueting Hall. There she removed her black gown to reveal a scarlet robe below. Her eyes were bound with the cloth in which the consecrated wafer had been wrapped. She then knelt upright and prepared to receive the sword blow, a royal privilege in France.

It was not to be. She was led to the block where three strokes of the axe were required to complete the deed.

When lifting her head the auburn hair came away in the executioner's hand. It was a wig revealing coarse grey below.

The long imprisonment had taken its toll. She was only 44 years old. Finally there was yet another surprise. Her little dog, faithful to the end, suddenly emerged from under her skirts and refused to budge from her side.

The body was then sealed in a lead coffin where it remained for six months. On the night of Sunday 30th July it was taken by torchlight procession through the twisting country lanes to

Peterborough Cathedral in readiness for the state funeral the following day.

Twenty five years later in 1612 her son, King James I, removed her body to Westminster Abbey where it lies to this day in a white marble tomb in the chapel of her grandfather Henry VII.

Signs of Fotheringhay's distinguished past are still visible. The beautiful church with flying buttresses and lantern tower can be seen rising above the landscape for miles around. The little room over a gateway in the main street where Bull is said to have stayed before the execution remains, as does the meagre pile of stones inside the iron railings. Below the massive grass mound the River Nene gently meanders. A scene full of atmosphere and melancholy on a grey winter day.

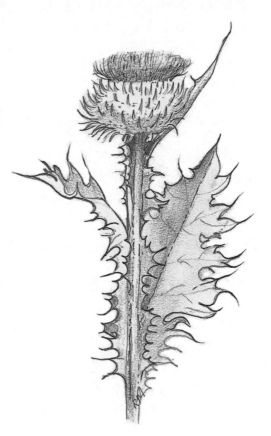

But those who love a dash of romance with their history will notice the huge thistles in the fields around the castle site and imagine them to be descendants of mythical forebears planted to provide the tragic Mary with reminders of her native Scotland.

6

"WITH HIS WHOLE HEART HE SANG SONGS"

In the centre of Great Billing a plaque affixed to the wall alongside the village noticeboard commemorates the life of "Our Beloved Squire".

Gervase Elwes 1866 - 1921.

One hundred yards up the hill the sign hanging outside the Elwes Arms appropriately portrays the family insignia and motto "Deo non fortuna", put faith in GOD not in fortune.

The cemetery of St Andrews Church, an attractive Norman building, contains many Elwes tombs.

But of Billing Hall, home to the family from 1795, nothing remains. The house has been demolished. Its grounds long built over. Lady Winifrede's Walk and Elwes Way, street signs on the housing estate to the east of the church, provide reminders of the past, and several gateposts and walls are decorated with the arrows and serpent depicted in the family coat-of-arms.

Looking towards the urban sprawl of modern Northampton it is difficult to realise that Robert, the first Elwes of Billing, exercised his racehorses on the Lings, "a pleasant covert with a straight mile from the main road and a circular mile around some fine Scotch pines".

Robert's heir Cary Charles Elwes squandered much of the family fortune. When he died in 1866, his son Valentine was bequeathed "a rifled house, a crop of debts and a hideous stepmother". Valentine had earlier escaped an unhappy home life by taking a commission in the Ninth Lancers and sailing away to fight in the Kaffir War. On leaving the army he travelled to Western Australia where his brother-in-law was Governor. During the return journey he met his first wife, Henrietta Lane, and for a time they had a house in Desborough. Henrietta died in 1864 but within two years Valentine had inherited Billing from his profligate father, and met and married Alice Ward, daughter of a Church of Ireland clergyman.

The night of November 14th 1866 was transfigured by showers of dazzling meteors and shooting stars. At 3 o'clock a particularly spectacular burst of heavenly fireworks heralded the birth of their first child, Gervase. Bells rang that morning as the people of Billing rejoiced with their Squire.

Eight years later however, noises from the church pulpit were much less friendly.

In common with other Victorian landed gentry the Elwes' frequently wintered abroad - Switzerland, Italy or Southern France. It was on one such visit to Nice that Valentine and his wife finally ended an agonising period of spiritual torment. They renounced Protestantism and were received into the

Roman Catholic Church. Hardly surprisingly this decision was not popular at home. In churches attached to the family's Lincolnshire estates at Roxby and Brigg, and particularly at Billing, clergymen made scathing attacks on Catholicism.

But the commotion was shortlived. "The friendliness between the family and all the tenants which had been a marked characteristic of Billing gradually re-established itself".

A lasting memorial to these events can be witnessed today in the main street.

The whitewashed Church of Our Lady of Perpetual Succour was constructed from a disused schoolroom in 1874 to provide a place of worship for the many villagers who followed their Squire into the Roman Church.

In 1877 Gervase and his brother Dudley were sent to the Oratory School at Edgbaston. Its founder, Cardinal Newman, encouraged a musical education and soon noted the boys' emerging talent. Gervase for the violin, Dudley the cello. Gervase enjoyed the music, was successful in athletics and excelled at cricket but was never really happy at school away from the peace of Billing and the affection of his parents. Fortuitously, a severe bout of pneumonia necessitated home nursing and resulted in a move at the age of 15, when he was admitted to Woburn Park School at Weybridge under the tutelage of Monsignor William Petre.

This unconventional establishment emphasising the virtues of self discipline and individual honour without the usual petty restrictions, was much derided by the educational establishment. It exactly suited Gervase, who responded positively to the paternal approach illustrated in a letter from Petre to Mr Cary Elwes.

"...... with large vivacious characters like his it is useless to attempt to force any special form upon him. The work is far more delicate. He must before all things be maintained in a sense of freedom and openness with all who have to deal with him".

At Woburn Park the boy developed qualities that shaped his character for the rest of his life.

In 1885 Gervase left school and went up to Christ Church College, Oxford. Here he met Lady Winifrede Fielding, whose father, the 8th Earl of Denbigh, had a house near the university. After a short courtship they became engaged. Winifrede recalls her first visit to Billing Hall on the occasion of her fiance's coming of age.

"..... our first view of Billing thrilled us, covered with wisteria blossom and standing surrounded by its glorious trees with rolling lawns running down to the string of ponds in the foreground.... the blaze of rhododendrons, the delicious smell of azaleas, and most of all the enchanting atmosphere of the place".

After their marriage on April 30th 1889 and honeymoon in Devon the couple returned to the village, entering the hall through a triumphal arch proclaiming "Hail the Bridegroom, Hail the Bride". The entire population were invited to inspect the presents before celebrating with a lavish tea in a barn on the estate.

Gervase had enjoyed little academic success at Oxford and left without a degree to enter the diplomatic service. This career took the growing Elwes family to Vienna and Brussels but it was not until their return to England to manage his ailing father's estates in Lincolnshire that Gervase began to cultivate and pursue an interest in singing which had first shown itself in Belgium. His personality, musicianship, temperament and good

"The first world war brought a temporary halt to globe-trotting. Gervase devoted himself to raising morale by giving concerts for the troops in France ....."

presence quickly impressed his teacher, Henry Russell, who recommended he try for a professional career. This was not the done thing! It was common for aristocratic Victorians to frown upon such self indulgence. The project caused consternation among his family and it was several years before his burgeoning reputation as a concert performer convinced them of the wisdom of his decision to follow Russell's advice.

His first professional engagement took place on Christmas Eve 1902. Gervase was well launched on a life of singing by 1909 when he inherited the Billing estate on his fathers death. He became established as one of the world's leading tenors making concert tours to many parts of Europe and the U.S.A., and enjoyed the friendship of such celebrated musicians as Percy Grainger, Sir Henry Wood and Ralph Vaughan Williams. His most famous role was the tenor lead in Elgar's "The Dream of Gerontius", which he sang on 118 occasions.

At the height of his fame he earned in excess of £2000 a year.

The first world war brought a temporary halt to globe-trotting. Gervase devoted himself to raising morale by giving concerts for the troops in France, well aware that his four eldest sons were on active service. Remarkably all survived. Geoffrey, the eldest, served in the Northamptonshire Yeomanry on the Western front and in Italy, Rolf saw action at Ypres, the Somme and Vimy Ridge and was decorated with the M.C. Cary spent three years as an intelligence officer in France and Val was at sea for the whole war period. Escaping from the stricken destroyer "Wolverine" he had arrived at Billing in borrowed clothes sizes too big, having lost all his possessions including gun, violin and kitten!

After the war Gervase successfully resumed his career and in the autumn of 1920 gave what were to be his final concerts in England.

The "Times" reported:

"Mr Gervase Elwes gave another of these recitals that made people wonder how it is a song can be so perfectly satisfying a thing".

Shortly afterwards he and his wife departed on the fateful trip to the United States and Canada. The tour began in Winnipeg, Christmas was celebrated in Washington, and then more concerts in New York before moving to Boston. On 12th January 1921 they left the train at Boston Back Bay Station. Gervase realised he'd mistakenly picked up the wrong coat and ran back to the carriage to return it. After throwing the coat to a conductor he slipped between platform and moving train, sustained dreadful injuries and died in hospital a few hours later.

In England there was a profound sense of shock at the news of his death. Obituaries were fulsome in their praise. The "Observer" wrote:

"The death of a great artist is an irreparable loss, but in the case of Elwes our loss is magnified over and over again by his purely personal qualities. He was one of those rare souls to whom ideals of art were indistinguishable or inseparable from ideals of living ......"

Fortunately recordings of his voice survive and an HMV Golden Voice Series L.P. was issued in 1968. Sadly the series did not include his "Dream of Gerontius".

In 1931 Geoffrey sold the estate and hall intending the house to become a home for retired musicians. After standing empty and desolate for many years and despite strenuous attempts to preserve the building, the bulldozers finally had their way in October 1956.

After Gervase's death the family continued to achieve distinction. Brother Dudley became the 5th Bishop of Northampton, son Cary an architect, Simon a portrait painter, Richard a high court judge and Valentine a Catholic priest and Naval Chaplain.

Grandson Mark trod the boards with Northampton Repertory Company and granddaughter Polly, married to Peter Dimmock, was a familiar T.V. personality in the 1950's.

In St Andrew's churchyard an inscription on the huge cross carved from Northamptonshire stone reminds us that Gervase left:

"to his wife and eight children the example of his faith, honour and kindness and to the world the memory of his voice".

On the plaque in the main street, below the impression of the great man's head in profile sculpted in bas relief by Arthur Vokes, whose studio had been at the bottom of the lawn at Billing Hall, is a similar message:

"With his whole heart he sang songs

And loved Him that made him."

7

TODAY WE'RE GOING TO DO POETRY

Do you remember when you were at school how, whenever it was very foggy or frosty or windy your teacher would announce,

"Today we're going to do poetry".

There would be groans around the room. It meant having to put on your coat and outdoor shoes to brave the weather. The

thick dense fog, the biting cold, the hair tugging wind. "Before you can write about it, you must feel it, touch it, taste it, experience it", the teacher would say. She was probably a John Clare fan. So what, you say. Who was John Clare? An unlikely poet if ever there was one.

He was born in the Northamptonshire village of Helpston near Peterborough in July 1793, the elder of two children. It was a typical village and his parents were typical villagers. Parker Clare, was a farm labourer crippled with rheumatism by the

41

age of forty. His father could read a little but neither of John's parents could write. The local schoolmaster encouraged his unusual love of books but schooling ended at the age of twelve when he had to find a job. Not that he was a stranger to work. Or to braving the weather.

From early childhood he would have helped with seasonal farming tasks. Crow scaring, weeding, stonepicking, sheep tending, threshing, winnowing, an endless list of hard work all the year round under fierce summer sun or in frost and snow. This was only the start. He now had to earn money to help support his parents and sister Sophy. He began by haymaking and learning to plough the fields around his home, or collecting dead sticks from the woods for firewood, or doing odd jobs and running errands.

Alas he wasn't a very good worker. He was a rather lazy boy and preferred his books to hard physical graft, which won him few friends amongst the villagers. Farm labourers weren't supposed to have ideas above their station.

But John Clare was no ordinary ploughboy. He possessed both a remarkable memory and fertile imagination. He wandered the woods, the heathland and the river banks around his Helpston home observing the countryside in minute detail. He noticed the frosted cobweb hanging like delicate lace on the hawthorn hedge, the unusual texture of an insect's skin, "the melancholy flapping" of a heron's wings. Keen eyes made daily discoveries. It was like "walking in a new world".

One day when Clare was thirteen years old there came about an exciting and revelatory experience. The village weaver happened to show him a tattered poetry book. "Seasons" by James Thomson. Overwhelmed by its contents John wanted a copy of his own and pestered his father for the eighteen pence (one fifth of his weekly wage) to buy it from a bookshop in

Stamford six miles away. When he arrived the book shop was closed. He'd forgotten it was Sunday. Shops didn't open on Sundays. The following morning he walked again into the town having bribed someone to look after his ploughing horses. At half past six he was sitting on the steps outside the bookshop waiting for it to open. The shopkeeper let him have the book for a shilling, and Clare set off back to Helpston. But he couldn't wait. As he passed the grounds of Burghley House he climbed over the stone wall into the park. It wasn't the done thing for a common labourer to be seen reading during working hours. Out of sight of the road he opened his book and began to read.

"Come gentle Spring, ethereal mildness come ...."

And read and read. He had forgotten the ploughing, forgotten everything. On that day he discovered poetry. The ideas and impressions stored away in his head since childhood found a voice. On the way back to Helpston he composed his first poem. "The Morning Walk".

He scarcely stopped writing from that first morning, and by the age of twenty one was producing six or seven poems a day. Dozens of these written on odd scraps of paper were secreted in an alcove by the fireside.

One morning his mother, either in ignorance or to deliberately punish her son for idling his time in "useless" scribbling, used them them to light the fire.

Eventually he decided his best poems deserved a more permanent home and visited a Market Deeping bookseller, John Henson, to get blank paper bound into a book. It was at this time while working fourteen hours a day as a labourer at a lime kiln at Bridge Casterton in Rutland, that Clare met Martha (Patty) Turner his future wife.

"What are riches? not worth naming

Though with some they may prevail

Theirs be choice of wealth prevailing

Mine be Patty of the Vale".

Perhaps inspired by this romantic association he renewed his contact with Henson in a bid to get into print. Eventually the bookseller agreed to produce for £1, three hundred prospectuses inviting subscribers for a small collection of "Original Trifles by John Clare". He was persuaded to write the prospectus himself,

".... the public are requested to observe that the trifles hereby offered for their candid perusal can lay no claim to eloquence of poetical composition ..."

One hundred subscribers were required to make publication viable. Despite Clare's vigorous distribution of the leaflets, only seven were forthcoming.

It was his lowest point. Having quarrelled with Patty and lost his job, he returned to Helpston, where he was forced to seek Parish Relief. He saw only one solution. To take the King's shilling and join the army. He was no soldier and this must have been a very last resort. Doubtless he recalled the event seven years earlier in 1812, when he had endured untold embarrassment and humiliation whilst enlisting in the militia during a Napoleonic "invasion" scare. His oversized uniform, clumsiness and discomfort with an unfamiliar weapon and general lack of physical co-ordination, brought the inevitable confrontation with an officer. Unable to ignore the endless sneers and taunts Clare struck the soldier and knocked him to the ground. Fortunately the incident never resulted in court martial and to his, and no doubt the population of Oundle's intense relief, the drunken rabble that passed for an army was disbanded and never called together again.

Perhaps while passing Burghley Park, the scene of his poetic awakening, the intense gloom lifted a little. Enough to provoke a visit to Patty Turner and achieve reconciliation.

His half hearted attempt to join the Royal Artillery at Stamford ended in rejection and he returned to Helpston where a surprise awaited. His prospectus had found an interested reader, Edward Drury of Stamford. Drury acquired the poems from Henson and after obtaining verification of their promise from Sir John English Dolben of Finedon, a literary man of some note, passed them to a relative. He was a London publisher by the name of John Taylor.

On January 16th 1820 the collection appeared under the title,

"Poems Descriptive of Rural Life and Scenery"

and begins:

> *"Hail humble Helpstone! where thy valley's spread*
>
> *And thy mean village lifts its lowly head*
>
> *Unknown to grandeur, and unknown to fame*
>
> *No minstrel boasting to advance thy name".*

The image of John Clare, Northamptonshire Peasant Poet was created in Taylor's introduction:

"The poems are the genuine productions of a young peasant, a day labourer in husbandry".

After the success of this first collection, Clare achieved a kind of fame. He was invited to London by rich patrons and received in the drawing rooms of the cultured and well-to-do.

For a short time he was pampered as a popstar or famous footballer might be treated today.

Clare dedicated his "Shepherd's Calendar", published in 1827 to:

"The most noble The Marquis of Exeter (Burghley House) In grateful remembrance of unmerited favours".

His preface states:

"I hope my low station in life will not be set off as a foil against my virtues".

Other local gentry, Earl Spencer and Earl Fitzwilliam, contributed to a fund for the permanent provision of the poet.

But gradually it all went sour. Clare never fitted into the world of high society. The tragedy was that his own people couldn't accept him either.

Financial troubles added to his problems. Little of the money made during that brief period of fame reached his pocket, and he now had a family of his own to support. Back in 1820 he had married Patty Turner and little more than a month after the wedding their first child was born. Although his wife proved a great source of support displaying the virtues of industry, frugality, good temper and love for her husband, she received scant reward. As public interest in his work declined Clare sank into acute depression. In 1837 he was admitted to a private hospital in Epping where he received treatment from an enlightened Doctor Allen, who provided a liberal environment for the disturbed poet. He was now suffering delusions, referring to his wife as Mary, (a Mary Joyce for whom he had shown a profound yet unrequited affection during his boyhood). After several attempted escapes he finally absconded from the institution in July 1841 and set out on foot to make the long journey back to his Northamptonshire home, without a penny in his pocket. He arrived, several days later, almost starving and near to exhaustion, to write in his journal:

"Returned home out of Essex, and found no Mary".

Poor Patty could not cope with his confused and disturbed condition and shortly afterwards allowed her husband to be committed to the Northampton Asylum.

Here he was treated with kindness and consideration, but inevitably this abandonment contributed to his melancholy.

After visiting Clare in the asylum in 1861 Kettering journalist, John Plummer, refers to him as "A forgotten poet". Clare's earliest biographer, Frederick Martin, writing in 1865, the year after his death, reports that "Patty never once showed herself in the twenty two years, nor any of her children, except the youngest son who came to see his father once".

Clare expressed his hurt in characteristic poetic eloquence:

"I am! Yet what I am who cares or knows?

My friends forsake me like a memory lost".

Wellingborough shoemaker and poet John Askham beautifully encapsulated Clare's sad demise in the last lines of a sonnet:

"Alas! we mourn thy fate, poor hapless Clare

That such a night should follow morn so fair".

Today John Clare's memorial can be found along with that of Shakespeare, Wordsworth and Keats in Poets Corner in Westminster Abbey. He is buried in Helpston churchyard next to his parents. An inscription reads:

"A Poet is born not made"

Perhaps so. But Clare believed that those childhood hours spent in the fields and woods around his home were the source of his wonderful words.

Which is why that enlightened teacher, looking out at the spring sunlight the snow or the wild wind would say:

"Today we're going to do poetry".

8

ANOTHER PILE OF STONES

The plumber laid his precious ladders on the quarry tiled floor, had one last look around the room and left the isolated cottage, locking the front door behind him.

"It can wait until Monday now," he thought. Everything will be safe and sound until then."

On the outskirts of Deenethorpe, about one hundred metres past the distinctive yew tree that stands in the middle of the street, a cluster of elms overhangs a steep bank above the Benefield Road. Scramble up the slope and you will find a pile of moss covered stones scattered amongst tangled roots and brambles. They have lain, undisturbed, since an icy December morning in 1943.

There was nothing unusual about the drone of aeroplanes in the skies above the village that day. No reason to lift heads from Sunday newspapers at breakfast tables. Late risers stirred momentarily in their sheets and turned over for ten minutes longer in bed. But ten minutes was all it would be.

Flying Fortresses from the 401st Bomb Group of the U.S.A.A.F. based at the aerodrome to the east of the village were taking off on a mission to Paris. Each carried six one thousand pound bombs. One by one the planes climbed slowly but surely above the rooftops. Now it was the turn of 42-39825 of 613 Bomber Squadron, quixotically christened by its crew, "Zenobia - E1 Elephante". Unable to gain sufficient height the huge plane swung off to the left and crashed full tilt into the unoccupied cottage on the edge of the village reducing it to a mass of rubble in seconds. On impact the bomber caught fire and eight of the ten crew members were able to scramble clear as the aircraft became enveloped in flames. Military Police from the camp were on the scene in seconds bravely dragging the navigator and bombardier from the wreckage.

The next few minutes were crucial. Realising that a huge explosion was imminent, the crew and police led by Sergeant John Rilko raced down to the village shouting "Hi! get out into the fields, our bombs may explode at any moment!"

Within seconds breakfasts were abandoned, newspapers discarded, lie-ins forgotten as villagers fled for their lives, some finishing their dressing as they ran. Eighty-two year old widow, Mrs Knighton was rescued by a neighbour, Albert Day who wrapped an overcoat around her and helped her to find shelter behind a mangold wurzle clamp. She was still wearing her slippers. Soon the entire population, minus one, about 100 men, women and children, were waiting breathlessly, fearful for themselves, their families, their homes and belongings.

Some lay flat, pressed to the frozen soil, others took cover behind haystacks, or crouched petrified in ditches.

Slowly the minutes passed until, BOOM! The bomb load was detonated by heat from the burning machine. Pieces of wreckage flung far and wide mingled with flying roots, hurtling tiles and splintered glass.

Not one of the 32 dwellings in Deenethorpe escaped damage. Every window was smashed and the noise of the explosion carried over half the county. Albert Day's house was almost demolished, furniture ruined and paper stripped off walls by the force of the blast. Yet the only fatalities were a calf and 14 fowls killed by an air screw blown through their shed about 50 metres from where the plane crashed. Amongst the injured were firemen from Kettering, buried when the walls of a cottage collapsed.

The only person to ignore the warnings was pensioner Charlie Adams who refused to leave the house where he lived alone. Fortunately he was unhurt.

It was nothing short of a miracle that no lives were lost. Although some villagers spread beds among the debris of their homes many were unable to return overnight, being accommodated in nearby Deene Park, Deene Rectory and Benefield village hall.

Most gratitude was reserved for the Eighth Army Airforce. Squire Brudenhall of Deene Hall commented that "the people of the village are still marvelling at the efficiency of you Americans. Saving our lives was wonderful ..... as was the food and bedding materials sent to those routed from their homes."

But the touch that really found favour was expressed by the village policeman.

"Now that we know no lives were lost we'd almost go through it again, for another shipment of oranges. We haven't seen one of those in years."

A window in Weldon Parish Church contains the stained glass image of Flying Fortresses which once adorned the camp chapel. On the Benefield to Weldon Road an inscribed granite stone pays tribute to air crew killed in action flying from Deenethorpe.

Yet in many ways a more poignant reminder of the village's place in recent history is provided by that pile of stones amongst the elm trees on the edge of a cornfield. And the memory of a plumber's ladders innocently stored for safe keeping in the cottage overnight.

9

THE MIND'S THE STANDARD OF THE MAN

Clothed in secrecy the carriage left the basement flat in London's Bedstead Square, a solitary occupant concealed within its depths and the blinds drawn. It was bound for Euston Station where a whole second class railway coach had been run into sidings, enabling the mysterious traveller to board unobserved, away from the departure platforms. Then, with curtains drawn, the reserved coach was shunted into the station to be attached to the mainline train. At Weedon the procedure was reversed and the anonymous passenger safely hidden in a cab for the final part of his journey.

His destination was Haycocks Hill Farm between Badby and Charwelton off the A361, and in the summer of 1887 part of the vast Knightley estate. In its secluded grounds he could satisfy a lifelong desire to "wander freely among fields, follow the windings of a wood, climb the brow of a breezy down or gather flowers in a meadow."

Our journey involved far less complex and elaborate travelling arrangements. We simply drove to Everdon, parked in the village and followed the footpath over the hill and down into the park. But then we weren't invited guests of Lady Louisa Knightley of Fawsley Hall and we certainly lacked the celebrity status of that earlier visitor. Joseph Merrick. Known to Victorian society and modern cinema audiences as The Elephant Man. Knightleys had lived at Fawsley since the early fifteenth century. In the Middle Ages wool represented the fastest possible shortcut to wealth, and the family amassed a tidy fortune by pulling down houses and evicting the inhabitants to create grazing land for sheep. They weren't alone. The Andrews at neighbouring Charwelton were in the same business. There, an eerily isolated church stands amongst grass grown mounds and hollow ways which hide the streets and buildings of a lost village. Go inside, lift a mat and discover the family's rise in status displayed in brass below - merchant, squire, gentleman and knight. The latter being an effigy depicting an armour clad Sir Thomas, his left foot resting symbolically upon a tiny sheep chewing on a sprig of clover.

The nearby hamlet of Snorscomb, and of course Fawsley itself, both met the same fate. Depopulated by sheep farming. Little wonder the desperate people cried "Sheep do eat up men."

Echoes of Captain Pouch? Resistance however, would have been futile. The justices of the peace were the very persons responsible for the evictions.

One, Edmund Knightley, a lawyer involved in the confiscation of property during Henry VIII's dissolution of the monasteries, built Fawsley Hall in 1540. Forty seven years later his nephew,

Sir Richard witnessed the execution of Mary Queen of Scots at Fotheringhay. Richard's own religious inclinations lay, not with the Established Church and its repressive Elizabethan bishops, but the emergent Nonconformist cause. An earnest Puritan he narrowly avoided a similar fate to the Scottish Queen when he became involved in the production and circulation of "The Marprelate Tracts", which virulently attacked the bigoted Anglican clergy.

According to romantic tradition the mobile press on which these publications were printed was housed in the little room above the glorious embattled Oriel window of the Great Hall, but Sir Richard himself at his trial, speaks of it having been concealed in the nursery.

(A newspaper article published shortly after Lady Louisa

Knightley's death in 1913 details the sale of paintings and artefacts from her collection. Amongst the items listed is a bound volume of two of the tracts, "The Epitome" and "The Epistle" which, as they "were being sold by public auction within a few yards of where they were printed secretly and with danger to the printer of arrest and death if discovered, was a romance of the auction room.")

In the event Sir Richard suffered a more lenient punishment than his fellows, several of whom were executed. After a brief period of imprisonment he was fined the huge sum of £10,000, although most of this was later abated thanks to discreet intercessions by powerful friends at Court. The family's nonconformist tradition continued into the next century when another Richard welcomed into the Fawsley vicarage a famous Puritan dissident, Doctor John Dod. His provocative and amusing sermons were always good value, none more than his celebrated condemnation of the evils of alcohol. The tale is told that in Cambridge one day he was waylaid by a gang of drunken University students and imprisoned in the stump of an ancient tree. These captors vowed never to release him until he had preached on the subject of "Malt." With considerable panache considering the circumstances, Dod began his sermon,

"Beloved, I am but a little man come at a short warning, to deliver a brief discourse upon a small subject to this thin congregation from an unworthy pulpit."

He then skilfully utilised the letters M.A.L.T. to introduce a series of exhortations, Moral, Allegorical, Literal and Theological, successfully demonstrating his hatred for the demon drink! John Wilkins, Dod's grandson, was briefly the incumbent at Fawsley in 1638 where he wrote a remarkable precursor of the space age entitled "The Discovery of a New World." His ideas were based upon his own astronomical observations, (He was a founder of the Royal Society), posing the possibility of another "habitable world in the moon" and the prospect of "a passage thither."

Yet another Richard succeeded to the estate in 1639. Civil war was imminent. The family's sympathies clearly lay with Parliament, indeed it is suggested that schemes for limiting the Royal Perogative were hatched at Fawsley Hall. It was certainly a rendezvous for Puritan leaders. Cromwell, Pym and Hampden were regular visitors and the latter's daughter Elizabeth eventually married into the Knightley dynasty.

Curiously Fawsley played an unwitting role in the outcome of the final decisive action of the war. Instead of consolidating a strong position prior to the Battle of Naseby, King Charles and his commanders hunted deer in this very park, unaware that the Parliamentarians were regrouping and about to regain the initiative. With the ensuing victory however the Knightley's remained constitutionalists rather than revolutionalists and, while ready to reduce the King's power, were not party to the decision to take away his life. In fact a fifth Richard was imprisoned for opposing Charles' arrest. Later restored to favour, during the Protectorate he served as Northampton-shire's M.P. from 1658 in Richard Cromwell's Parliament, and was a member of the council which decided to recall Charles II two years later.

Approaching Fawsley from Everdon it is difficult to determine where countryside ends and parkland begins. What a tribute to the foresight and genius of Capability Brown.

Over two hundred years ago he created a landscape which today blends harmoniously with the surrounding fields and woods. Nestling beneath one ancient tree is a tumbled down building, half stone, half brick. A dower house built in the early

16th century by Sir Edmund Knightley for his widow Ursula. The plaque screwed to crumbling masonry invokes an Ancient Monuments Act to preserve the ruin against despoilation.

Legislation alone offers no protection against the ravages of time or the creeping ivy that clings so tenaciously to its walls and mullioned windows. A single surviving Tudor chimney twists elegantly sky-wards.

No Knightley widow ever resided there after Richard's second wife Anne, who outlived her husband by over forty years.

From her death in 1702 until the end of the century the building was occupied by estate workers, since when it has stood, empty and desolate in its isolation. The avenue of elms which once led the short distance over the hill to the hall have long since succcumbed to age and disease.

On Anne's death wooden panels are believed to have been removed from the house and installed in nearby St Mary's Church.

Their decoration depicts "Hey diddle diddle." A familiar children's nursery rhyme. Or does it? Not necessarily. A rather fanciful interpretation suggests the carvings represent a clever, but treasonable allegory originating from the reign of Richard III. Cats and fiddles, cows and moons, little laughing dogs and dishes and spoons were all symbols for the leading players in Richard's seizure of the throne in 1483.

Queen Victoria's tenure was more secure. One of her grooms-in-waiting Sir Thomas Bowater raised a family in the Queen's house at Richmond. His daughter Louisa became a member of the court and close to several of Victoria's children. Her journals recall as commonplace encounters with "royal personages". In 1869 she married Sir Rainald Knightley. Lord Knightley represented his South Northants constituency in

Parliament for an unbroken forty years. Cynics were not impressed with his contribution however, insinuating that his credibility relied too much upon privileged ancestry. As one wit observed, "Knightley to the listening earth, repeats the story of his birth."

There is little doubt that his wife was the power behind his political career and the true source of whatever popularity he enjoyed locally. Regarded as the leading lady in the public life of the county her interests were extensive - political, philanthropical, educational, historical and religious. She was freely acquainted with the great and powerful. Her journals inform us that at one party she "walked up the steps with Disraeli and down with Gladstone". Yet she also possessed the common touch. Toryism, the natural persuasion of Victorian landed gentry, was tempered with genuine compassion.

Indicative is a journal entry made when canvassing for Sir Rainald in Towcester during the election campaign of 1885.

"Some very radical shoemakers in some horrid little courts down at the bottom of the town. I should be a Radical *myself* if I lived in such holes."

Lady Louisa was a great believer in the capacity of women and was associated with a large number of organisations which promoted opportunities for girls. Foremost were her involvement with the Emigration League which enabled young women to travel to distant colonies, South Africa and Canada, to begin new lives in service, and the "Girls Friendly Society" which looked after the social and moral welfare of working girls at home.

Modern day cynicism may well cast Louisa Knightley in the role of Lady Bountiful but this would fail to acknowledge contemporary accounts of the universal affection with which she was held. Reporting her funeral, "The Independent"

"I would be measured by my soul
The mind's the standard of the man."

records "the loss of this beloved lady was shared by Royalty: by national and local societies, by young and old of all classes of society ...."

Lady Louisa is buried in St Mary's churchyard alongside her husband. Their marriage was childless.

Had he lived beyond his paltry 29 years no doubt Joseph Merrick would have joined the impressive list of mourners at her funeral, albeit from a respectful distance and in a guise guaranteed to protect their sensibilities. Rescued from a miserable existence in a fairground freak show by eminent surgeon Sir Frederick Treves, the Elephant Man was admitted to the London Hospital in 1886. He had suffered from birth from multiple neuro fibromatosis, which rendered him perhaps "the most hideously deformed creature ever known." The Chairman of the Hospital management committee described his new patient as "so dreadful a sight that he is unable even to come out by daylight to the garden .... women and nervous persons fly in terror from the sight of him." Yet it was soon apparent to those who became sufficiently acquainted that he was "superior in intelligence, could read and write, was quiet, gentle, not to say even refined in his mind." It was these qualities, and no doubt a peculiar fascination, that attracted ladies of society to his basement flat at the hospital. Amongst them was Lady Knightley, who persuaded Merrick to holiday on her Northamptonshire estate. On his second visit in 1888 he stayed at Red Hill Farm near Byfield where he was befriended by a thirteen year old farm worker, Walter Steel. In the Daventry Express of May 1981 Steel's nephew recalls his uncle speaking of Merrick's talent for writing poetry and his lovely singing voice.

Further evidence of this sensitivity appears in the autobiographical notes circulated with a handbill advertising his fairground appearances. Merrick concludes, "In making my first appearance before the public, who have treated me well, in fact I may say I am as comfortable now as I was uncomfortable before, I must now bid my kind reader adieu."

He then borrows inaccurately but so poignantly, from Isaac Watts, the celebrated seventeenth century clergyman and poet:

"Were I so tall, could reach the pole

Or grasp the ocean with a span

I would be measured by my soul

The mind's the standard of the man."

There is little doubt that the peace and tranquillity of those Fawsley holidays brought respite from the "boxed in" confinement Merrick endured in London. Sadly he was found dead in his London rooms one afternoon, just six months after a third visit in 1889. Doctors found difficulty in explaining the circumstances that led to his death, apparently through asphyxiation, and various theories were put forward. Sir Frederick Treves' account is widely regarded as the definitive version and contains an explanation consistent with Merrick's pathetic desire to "be like other people. Apparently Joseph's normal method of sleeping was, "to sit up in bed with his back supported by pillows, his knees drawn up, and his arms clasped round his legs, while his enormous head rested on the points of his bent knees." He had often told Treves that he wished to lie down to sleep as others did. The surgeon believed that on that fateful afternoon he experimented and lay back, causing his large, heavy head to topple from the soft pillow. Death was caused by dislocation of the neck.

Treves' high regard for Merrick is demonstrated in his account of the Elephant Man's life. Writing of their first meeting he described Joseph as "the most disgusting specimen of humanity he had ever seen." Later he wrote more discerningly that "the spirit of Merrick, if it could be seen in the form of the living, would assume the figure of an upstanding and heroic man ......"

On Louisa's death the estate had passed to her nephew Sir Valentine Knightley and subsequentley to Sir Charles Knightly whose death in 1932 virtually ended the family connection with Fawsley. The estate passed by marriage to the present owners the Gage family. Except for the hall. This escaped the fate of many other in the county although for several years its survival hung in the balance.

In "Portrait of Northamptonshire" P E Webb describes the "dereliction of the buildings ...... the curiously desolating silence which hangs over an untenanted house like a pall."

After occupation by army units during both world wars the hall entered perhaps the most bizarre period of its long and distinguished history. The "Timken Times" of April 1958 curiously informs that "Where Cromwell, Pym and other great figures of the days of Parliamentary rule once dined, are stacks of wooden planks." These planks were made from the wood of ancient trees felled in the park and taken to the hall to be transformed into export packing cases housing tapered roller bearings from factories in Duston and Daventry. The article further describes how "saws buzz and hammers keep up an industrious tattoo in the long, gracious ballroom where once bewigged gallants led their ladies in the minuet and gavotte." This decorous prose merely adds insult to the commercial vandalism wreaked upon the great house, as do the photographs of "majestic trees now being made into packing cases."

However in 1975 the "Chronicle and Echo" rejoiced in the news that Fawsley Hall was "to be restored to something like its former glories." A wealthy antiques dealer acquired the building for £30,000, later spending almost a quarter of a million pounds to transport a landscaped garden 350 miles from the Glasgow Garden Festival as a present for his wife.

Such restoration is indeed creditable. But what would Capability Brown make of it all, this instant prefabricated splendour? Not very much I suspect. Yet when surveying the legacy of his own work around the acres of parkland he might allow himself just the smallest smile of self satisfaction, after all it has served his reputation well for over 250 years.

10

"DEAR DAY GOODBYE"

"………. Matthews seemed to beat the entire Bolton left flank and then the perfect low cross was over to the middle and Perry whipped it into the net. A few mad seconds later the whistle went …….."

This description of Blackpool's winning goal in the cup final appears in the F.A. Book for Boys for 1953. But who was the author?

Perhaps in reflecting upon the part played by the great Stanley Matthews the writer may have been thinking back to his own footballing capabilities as described in a school magazine article of 1920.

"Our most dangerous forward, is very fast, shoots well but should learn to centre more often instead of relying on a shot from a difficult angle."

A further clue to the writer's identity appears in that same magazine, his first published poem entitled "Armistice Day", while the 1921 edition contains yet more significant references.

A second poem, "Evening" and "An appreciation of John Clare: Peasant Poet."

Interestingly enough there is also a cricketing review which concludes, "Special mention of Mr E E Kirby who, though sadly incapacitated through wounds received in the "Great Game" has always been willing to give his services when opportunity has allowed."

This was the very same Edmund E Kirby who, sixty seven years later, (in a foreword to Peter Eads' expansive bibliography), recalled "his lifelong friendship" for the schoolboy winger with literary ambition. H.E.BATES.

A plaque on the wall of a terraced house in Grove Road, Rushden, denotes where Herbert Ernest, (names he deplored), was born on May 16th, 1905.

From the first volume of his autobiography, "The Vanished World", we can detect the two major influences that shaped his early writing. One being the fields, hedgerows, woods and streams explored on golden afternoons with his grandfather Lucas, who taught him the minutiae of the countryside. The other, the mean streets of the town where, "some shoemaking dictator had insisted that for every hundred yards of dwelling house there should be thirty or forty of factory sandwiched between and then had added the humanitarian proviso that a bakehouse and a chapel or two should be tucked in among them."

The flavour of Bates' childhood, honeyed rural delicacies and bitter industrial gall, can be captured in his stories. "The Watercress Girl" is a hugely romantic evocation of an idyllic world full of sun, streams, wheat, flowers and strange colourful relatives, while "The Barber" recreates the plight of two boys waiting in a corner shop for a haircut, amongst intimidating, rough and vulgar shoeworkers.

Every weekday morning the boy woke to the sound of feet in the street outside "hurrying, running ...... scratting, to work in boot factories......"

His father, a clicker at Knight and Lawrence's in Manton Street not far from home, was determined that his son should avoid the all too common route from school to factory.

Albert Bates had aspirations towards something more genteel. Fortunately H.E.'s education was gloriously enhanced by encounters with two remarkable teachers who ensured that his talents were nurtured and encouraged. At Newton Road school he met Mrs Hensman who conveyed to the boy her own passion for art, English and music. On transferring to Kettering Grammar School he was eventually rescued from what he described as a miserable existence by the inspirational Edmund Kirby. The school master later recalled the debt **he** owed to the fourteen year old Bates. Apprehension at taking over from the timid women and old gents who had held the reins during hostilities was increased by his lack of teaching experience and a harrowing war. But in the boy from Rushden he recognised a responsive, keen and sensitive pupil, "the mainstay of the form", who helped to transform completely the class'.

The feeling was mutual. Of his first lesson with the young ex-infantry officer Bates writes, "If it is possible to change human vision or at best waken it, by the stimulus or even shock of a single experience, then this is the perfect example of it ...... fanciful as it might sound, I date my literary career from that moment."

While sport and literature dominated school life his social world centred upon a small circle of friends, bicycle rides, tennis, walks or "lolling around Wicksteed Park."

He left school on December 21st 1921 forsaking the opportunity of a university place. The reason is enigmatically described on his record card as "with his father", but in fact he took a position as "very junior" assistant reporter at the "Northampton Chronicle" in Wellingborough. For ten shillings (50p) a week he sampled the joys of the "provincial journalistic roundabout."

Hardly surprisingly he soon tired of this routine, finding little scope to indulge his literary ambitions whilst reporting an endless catalogue of fetes, garden parties, flower shows and regattas, and resigned a few months later.

There were unexpected bonuses however. Several characters and incidents from that period appear, thinly disguised in later stories. An assignment to interview the occupants of Rushden Hall and the single, momentary observation of a "tallish, dark, proud, aloof young girl in a black cloak lined with scarlet" climbing from a pony drawn gig at Rushden station, resurface in the hauntingly atmospheric "Love for Lydia", written some thirty years later.

Some weeks after leaving The Chronicle he began work in a warehouse in Griffiths Street. The business supplied odds and ends to the shoe trade: eyelets, threads, laces, tacks, rivets, wax, glue etc. H.E. completed his daily tasks of book-keeping, ordering and packaging in a matter of hours, leaving the rest of the day in which to write. In these remarkable circumstances he completed poems for a weekly magazine, "The Kettering Reminder" and a play "Loyalty", (advertised as 'Have we got talent in Rushden?'), which was later performed at the Co-operative Hall in March 1926. It was here that he also completed his first novel "The Two Sisters."

A few days before Christmas 1925 he received a letter from the publishers Jonathan Cape, the tenth to whom he'd sent manuscripts, expressing a wish to publish the book.

On June 24th the following year 1500 copies were printed at

".....leaving the rest of the day in which to write."

7/6d (37p). In its foreword the well known novelist and reviewer Edward Garnett describes the story as "A novel of rare poetical order ...... remarkable in an author of twenty years".

To write a second novel of equal quality proved more demanding and Bates, as ever lacking self confidence, became disheartened. In response to one submission Garnett wrote, "I am very glad you sent it to me for it would harm you to print it ..... it's really like a novice .... and from you!"

Once again the young writer was rescued from the depths of depression by a fortunate encounter, this time at a party at Manor Farm, Higham Ferrers. Here in February 1927 he met "a demure, attractive girl with a very striking pink and white complexion," Marjorie (Madge) Cox. Four years his junior she worked sewing uppers in one of the town's shoe factories from 7.30a.m. - 5.30p.m. Despite the apparent differences in their interests, the romance blossomed, leading to marriage in July 1931 at Rushden's Park Road Methodist Church. Friends described Madge Bates as the perfect wife for H.E., "making his writing possible by creating an island of stability and calm in which he could work". They left Northamptonshire to make their home in a converted granary at Little Chart near Ashford in Kent.

Here they indulged a mutual passion for gardening, and brought up a family, while Bates continued the struggle to establish his literary career. At the outbreak of war in 1939, despite his reputation as a gifted short story writer, he was still not a profitable author.

The relationship with his publisher became strained. He wrote "I am constantly being told that I am the finest short story writer in England but I don't seem to engender the same confidence in you."

He was certainly prolific. Twenty books were produced between 1925 and 1940 but critics were beginning to observe a "rather tired quality" in his work. A new direction was required.

This came with a much needed stroke of luck in 1941. As the war dragged on with little indication that the tide was turning Bates was commissioned to write short stories describing the vital role of the R.A.F.

Known as Flying Officer X he was attached to fighter and bomber stations throughout the country with a brief to get close to the serving man. He resolved however, to be an artist first and a propagandist second. It was with some reluctance that Jonathan Cape agreed a deal with the Air Ministry but in the event the books were a phenomenal success.

"There's something in the air," and "How sleep the brave" captured the spirit and character of the R.A.F., selling in hundreds of thousands and boosting morale. A dispute over royalties, (Bates received a pittance for these books), led to the inevitable rift with Cape and an advance on a new novel was agreed with Michael Joseph. Bates writes, "After twenty years of writing, with its several disasters and constant struggles, "Fair stood the wind for France", was my first wide success."

The book was published in November 1944 and expressed through its lovers Frankie and Francoise the hope that a younger generation raised on war and aware of the evils of hate may yet build a better world. Little wonder that it sold so well. (The book was serialised by B.B.C. television in 1980 and a dramatised version, adapted by Gregory Evans and Michael Napier Brown had its world wide premiere at Northampton's Royal Theatre in 1986).

In February 1945 Bates left for the Far East. This assignment provided inspiration for such postwar novels as "The Purple Plain", "The Jacaranda Tree" and "The Scarlet Sword". But in 1952 he returned to his Northamptonshire roots with "Love for Lydia". Regarded by many as his most satisfying and aesthetically complete novel the story leans heavily upon the writer's experiences as a young man. Even the distant Mrs Hensman appears in a walk on part as a therapist in Evensford's sanatorium.

"Mrs Montague, a tallish, sallow skinned, spare woman of sixty, with rimless spectacles, who had taught me as a child, came up to the bed with strips of flowered petit point in her hand ..."

This renewal of links with his home town was extended in 1955, the year of his fiftieth birthday, when H.E. accepted an invitation to become an honorary vice president of Rushden Cricket Club. (An event which led to fixtures between his adopted Kentish village and Rushden which were much enjoyed for several seasons).

Yet fittingly it was at a football match, another F.A. cup final, that H.E. first alluded to his most popular creation. The game was in the doldrums with little to excite spectators. Suddenly, to the huge embarrassment of his companion, printer Ken Geering, Bates let out a mighty guffaw, laughing uncontrollably.

"What's wrong?" his friend implored, fearing for the author's sanity.

Recovering sufficiently H.E. replied, "I'm going to write a book".

"So what? You're always writing books."

It appeared that a lorry piled high with scrap metal had parked outside the village store a few days previously. Down from its cab climbed a wiry father, a huge mother and hordes of happy, excited children. They all piled into the shop, to emerge shortly after licking at gigantic ice-creams and eating from bags of crisps. Wiping dollops of vanilla ice from his red face the father announced to the world at large, "Perfick wevver ma!"

In that moment Pa Larkin was conceived.

Bates was entitled to laugh aloud. In "The Darling Buds of May" and its successors, he indulges a love of the country-side, portrayed so vividly in his many naturalist publications and invents wonderfully comic characters.

He later described the books as, "English as pubs, steak and kidney pudding and the Canterbury Tales of Chaucer". The series certainly brought him a new readership in the late fifties much as the recent hugely successful T.V. adaptation has freshly acquainted a younger generation with the riotous doings of the Larkin family.

Evidence of his lifelong friendship with Edmund Kirby is again revealed in 1969 when, encountering difficulties with his story "The Triple Echo", later filmed with Glenda Jackson and Oliver Reed, Bates again turned to his old teacher for advice.

There were problems relating to ballistics and the shotgun used by a key character. Who better to consult than the former infantry officer?

In June 1973 Bates was awarded the C.B.E. but sadly, shortly before Christmas that year, he was admitted to hospital in Canterbury and died of kidney failure and related complications on January 29th 1974. At a service of thanksgiving at St Bride's Church, Fleet Street Sir Bernard Miles read the famous passage on Charity from Corinthians.

An obituary in the "Times" maintains that H.E. Bates "stood in the direct line of succession of fiction writers of the English countryside that includes George Eliot, Hardy and D.H. Lawrence." Splendid company indeed, but I still prefer the second verse of that so early poem, written as a sixteen year old for the Kettering Grammar school magazine:

> *"Let the purple of even fade away*
>
> *White grows the road*
>
> *Beneath the moonlit sky:*
>
> *Home goes the wanderer to his own abode*
>
> *Dear day goodbye".*

11

RAMBLES ROUNDABOUT

I was introduced to the De Wildes by accident in a second hand book shop. A brief synopsis of the lives of Samuel and his son George James appears in the catalogue of an exhibition, held at the Central Art Gallery in Northampton during the Autumn of 1971. I was intrigued and that chance acquaintance led me on a journey of exploration following the younger De Wilde's "Rambles Roundabout" Northampton-shire.

It began on a chill December afternoon. I found myself at the small village of Barnwell, not far from Oundle in the far north of the county. George De Wilde described Barnwell All Saints as "one of those by-way stations which only the slow trains discover."

The Old Station House still stands on a corner plot where the Barnwell road leaves the busy A605, but nothing save an abandoned goods van in a nearby field even suggests the existence of a railway line, let alone a station. I re-read De Wilde who, borrowing words from Edmund Spenser, quotes

"Far removed from pomp and riot

And the busy hum of men."

But he was writing one hundred and thirty years ago and times change. I discovered that the track now lies buried beneath the ribbon of tarmac that carries speeding motor traffic between Oundle and Thrapston. Pondering this fact, and the solitary station house, I sought the missing building making enquiries in the village.

"Follow the road to Elton, go on past Sibson aerodrome, cross the A1 and you can't miss it! It's at Wansford." Bewildered I tried to imagine how George de Wilde would have felt. Undaunted I set off on the trail, only to discover further surprises were in store.

There indeed was Barnwell Station. The "small, picturesque and unpretentious building" offering the fortunate station-master "time for thought and tranquil enjoyment" stood masked by a white canopy. Part of its "snug indoor shelter for winter travellers", utterly transformed like a theatre set, with fake snow, tinsel and glitter, to create Santa's grotto, where passengers gathered before boarding for a seasonal train ride to Peterborough and back. I am sure George de Wilde would have regarded the improbable scene with characteristic good humour. It may have evoked memories of his own unusual childhood, while as a devoted family man he might even have relished the fun of the Santa Specials. But the conservation of the station, so lovingly dismantled board by board, transported from its original home and recreated at Wansford by the Peterborough Railway Society would certainly have gained approval. After all, had he not in later years been preoccupied with founding a museum in his own Northampton?

The de Wildes had originally arrived in England from Holland during the early 18th century, eventually settling in London's St Giles-in-the-Fields. George's grandfather died prematurely in 1753 increasing financial pressures on the family and at fourteen his father Samuel became apprenticed to an uncle's joinery firm. He did not complete indentures however, becoming in 1769 the sixty seventh student to enrol at the newly formed Royal Academy Schools.

Samuel developed remarkable skills as a portraitist, exhibiting for the first time at the Academy in 1781. Between 1792 and his "retirement" thirty years later rarely a year passed without his work being shown.

It was during this period that he established a reputation as the leading theatrical portrait painter, achieving an almost complete monopoly of the trade. His work, featuring many of the great actors and actresses of the time consistently appeared in leading publications. From his studio in Tavistock Row he circulated among London's great theatres. Covent Garden, Drury Lane, the Lyceum in the Strand and the Little Theatre in the Haymarket.

Samuel's drawings now grace the Royal collection at Windsor and a large number still adorn the walls of the Garrick Club, bearing further testimony to the quality of his work. Yet despite a prolific output and unrivalled reputation he enjoyed little financial security or the wider recognition he felt he deserved. It was into such a colourful yet precarious background that George James de Wilde was born in 1804, the elder of two children.

He grew up surrounded by artistic paraphernalia and imbibed the atmosphere of London's theatres. Unsurprisingly he was "originally destined to be an artist", and a boyhood sketch-book demonstrates his early promise as a draughtsman. His formal, classical education was limited, however George did develop a love of letters, becoming through theatre connec-tions intimately acquainted with Leigh Hunt and other notable literary personages of the day.

At the age of twenty one he took a temporary secretarial post at the Colonial Office, where his outstanding abilities and diligence attracted the attention of Sir James Stephen, Assistant Secretary for the Colonies. Stephen's sister had married Thomas Edward Dicey, a member of the newspaper publishing family which had owned of all things the "Northamp-ton Mercury" since its foundation in 1720. When a vacancy occurred in Northampton, for his own good reasons Stephen recommended De Wilde, then only twenty four, for the position of editor. He retained the post until the day of his death over forty years later.

In modern terminology he was a "workaholic" seldom leaving the Mercury offices except on editorial business. There he earned the respect and admiration of all, for as Edward Dicey recalls, "he never wrote or said an unkind word, never lost a friend or made an enemy, never asked a favour or refused a service."

In 1825 he had married Mary Butterworth and was determined to provide a more secure family life for his children than he had enjoyed himself. Sadly his wife died in 1841 shortly after the birth of a fifth child, who also succumbed only months later. Distraught De Wilde promptly immersed himself in his work, widening his interests in civic affairs to include support for the town's Mechanics Institute, for whom in the same year he promoted a fund raising exhibition at Northampton. He supplied from his personal collection paintings, curiosities, artefacts and autographs of such famed figures as Words-worth, Byron and his old acquaintance Leigh Hunt, with whom he still corresponded.

De Wilde's own literary output was largely restricted to editorial duties, but he found time to contribute items to a number of publications including "The Gentlemen's Magazine" and "Notes and Queries" under a variety of imaginative non-de-plumes such as Sylvan Southgate, Camden Somers and Vandyke Brown.

"Rambles Roundabout" were not written for publication as a complete work, but were originally published at various intervals and over a period of years in The Mercury. After De Wilde's death they were collated into a concise volume of articles and poems by Edward Dicey, son of his proprietor and friend who wrote a fulsome introduction to the book entitled "In Memoriam". (Interestingly their editorship was disputed by one Samuel Smith Campion, De Wilde's chief reporter and later himself the proprietor and editor of the Mercury from 1885-1905. He claimed that his own contribution in editing the book received no acknowledgement or even thanks from Dicey).

The "Rambles" record summer holiday visits to locations around the county. Blisworth, Gayton, Rothersthorpe, Cotter-stock et al, apparently a random choice, but all accessible in those days by rail. The style is elegant. Classical, historical and anecdotal references blend comfortably with lyrical obser-vation. The following delightful yet poignant example from the previously quoted article on Barnwell draws attention to a monument in the Mortuary Chapel of All Saints church at the southern extremity of the village.

"Beneath a pyramid of alabaster, profusely covered with the armorial bearings of the Montagues, duly blazoned, in an arch which over canopies the figure of a child in the costume of the

"The memorial to the infant Henry proved quaint and fanciful."

aristocracy of two centuries and a quarter ago is the inscription.

"Obiit, proh dolor, immature per aquas 28th April 1625".

And beneath,

"Hereunder lyeth interred Henry Montague Esq..... a little and hopeful child, tender and dear in the sight of his parents, and much lamented of his friends."

The story is that the poor child, who was but three years old, fell into the moat while he was reaching an orange which he had dropped into the water and was drowned."

De Wilde was surely remembering his own daughter Alice, a child of his second marriage, who also died young in 1852, aged only four.

Braving Arctic weather I followed the writer's trail through Barnwell village to find this chapel that houses the remains of twenty-nine members of the Montague family. The porchway of a neighbouring bungalow provided welcome respite from driving rain as I waited to collect the key. Then it was a quick dash into the churchyard. For a few brief moments sleet turned to snow and the strange, truncated building appeared, ghostly through a white swirl of flakes, bringing to mind lines from a De Wilde poem,

".... today,

Winter. In one fierce night the yellow plains

Are whitened, and the rivulets pleasant way

Is stayed."

These words offered a timely reminder of the date.

December 23rd.

Inside, the memorial to the infant Henry proved as "quaint and fanciful" as described. Particularly unusual are the pair of human feet which support the upper part of the monument. They are immersed in water which gushes from a replica village pump and bear the words "Not my feet only, but also my hands and head" with supplication that "The joys of thy salvation pour on me."

Hugely impressed, on returning home I consulted Arthur Mee for the sculptor's name. It was a renowned Jacobean carver of statuary. Gerard Christmas!

The Rambles were not confined to distant rural locations. Among the more interesting are impressions of Abington, Kingsthorpe, Weston Favell and of the Drapery in the very centre of Northampton itself. He observes,

"The fashion is extending of separating the domestic establishment from the house of business, and bye-the-bye possibly, everyman, at the close of the day will lock all his cares up in his warehouse and go to his home and family a cheerfuller if not a wealthier man for the change."

Not that De Wilde escaped very far from his own workplace. He and *his* family remained above The Mercury offices in the Parade.

De Wilde's interest in the arts continued to flourish, particularly during the eighteen sixties. John Askham, the Wellingborough shoemaker and poet, was one to benefit from this patronage. When his work first appeared in the Wellingborough Independent De Wilde was impressed and helped Askham supplement his income by appointing him Wellingborough correspondent of The Mercury. He likened his verse to that of John Clare whose confinement in the Northampton Asylum coincided with much of De Wilde's tenure.

Fittingly "Rambles Roundabout" contains a sensitive tribute to the great poet, including a splendid example of the country-man's acute discomfort in high society.

"When he became for a time a wonder in the fashionable world he was bewildered, and when dinner was over he would rise, thrust his hands in his pockets and saying "Well I'll goo - goo accordingly."

Although De Wilde was only an adoptive son of the county, his words display sympathetic affection for Clare's characteristic lapse into broad local dialect.

Unbelievably he left Northamptonshire in 1871 for the first time since arriving from London some forty years earlier. Even then it was only to seek relief from an illness that struck with sudden ferocity during the spring of that year. He recovered sufficiently to resume work, but sadly died at The Mercury's offices on September 16th, shortly after correcting proof sheets for the forthcoming edition of his newspaper.

And so one hundred years later, on the anniversary of his death, we come to the exhibition at Northampton Central Art Gallery. This celebration of the lives and works of the De Wildes, a remarkable father and son, had started my quest. Fittingly too, that July in Highgate cemetery, another devotee, the vicar of Highgate, had resurrected a gravestone from under a foot of earth. It recorded the burial place of none other than George De Wilde, his first wife Mary and daughters Florence and Alice, who both died in infancy.

Edward Dicey provides an appropriate tribute.

"No human being, to the best of my belief, was ever the worse for having known George James De Wilde: there were few who were not better for the knowledge: and than this I know of no higher and I can add no truer epitaph."

Cotterstock Church

12

NEGLECTED, DESPISED AND FORGOT

Bath, Buxton, Tunbridge Wells, Leamington Spa, Wellingborough. You might well ask what Wellingborough is doing on such a list. The clue is in the name.

Evidence of ancient habitation in the area around the Ise tributary to the north of the town, was unearthed during construction work on the Queensway estate during the nineteen sixties. An Iron Age hut circle containing the skeletons of members of the Coritani tribe was discovered there above the ancient trackway now known as Brickhill Road.

But a first recorded name for the settlement dates from Saxon times when it was referred to as "Waendelburgh", the town of Waendel's people. In the Domesday Book (1086) it is called both Wendlesberie and Wendlingberic while various other corruptions occurred throughout the Middle Ages. In the early seventeenth century however the town became known as Wellingborrow or more commonly, Wellingborough. Contemporary writers attributed the change of name to the abundance of wells, fountains and springs in the district. Hundreds existed in the town and, in 1830, no less than 35 wells were recorded within a space of four hundred yards of the Cannon Street area. Some names survive to this day - Whytewell, Hollywell, Hemmingwell. One, however, was pre-eminent. The famed Red Well. It was thought at one time that its name was derived from the medieval term "Rodewellenor" or "Reed Spring Hill".

Situated immediately above the well itself was a piece of ground, probably a pond or swamp with no doubt an abundance of aquatic vegetation. However the common explanation suggests that the name originated from the red deposit left by its water on the stones and earth over which it flowed.

Its celebrated status dates from occasions when, as John Askham, Wellingborough's shoemaker, schoolmaster, journalist and poet recalls,

> *"A Royal pair once with their kingly court*
>
> *Visited Redwell and drank the healing stream*
>
> *Pitching their tents in the warm summer beam ...."*

The Royal pair were no less than King Charles I and his Queen, Henrietta Maria who visited the town with the express purpose of taking the chalybeate or sparkling spa water that gushed from the spring.

Writing in 1740, almost a century after their visits, in an essay on the principles of mineral waters, Thomas Short M.D. described Chalybeate as "a water impregnated with particles of iron or steel, these metallic particles give the blood fresh

"A Royal pair once with their kingly court visited Redwell ...."

momentum or force, hence this usefulness in all fissyness, poorness and thickness of our juices in a languid circulation, sluggishness and restiness of the vessels". Truly a panacea of great value and delight for that or any other age!

Such waters were much in vogue during the seventeenth century. Sir Theodore Mayern, their Majesties physician who probably accompanied the couple to Wellingborough recommended the Red Well in his writings. His views were supported by one Doctor Murret, who held it in high regard and placed it alongside the foremost "Purging waters of England". Certainly the increasing reputation of these "medicinal" waters induced the King and his retinue to spend lengthy periods in Wellingborough in 1628 and 1637. Tradition maintains that the whole court lived in tented pavilions erected in fields adjoining the spring. It is more likely that they were quartered overnight in the town, with Charles and his queen residing at "The White Swan", a hostelry which then stood in the Market Place. This ancient inn, apparently more luxurious in those days than its better known counterpart, The Hind Hotel, was favoured with a finely carved oak chimney piece containing a Royal monogram surmounted by a crown, and a portrait of Henrietta Maria, which gives credibility to this view. Sadly both relics disappeared, on the demolition of the building in 1829.

Ancient Church and Town ledgers confirm that levies were made on account of the two visits, and Henry and Thomas Hensman, John Glendon and Paul Dennett are named as beneficiaries, reimbursed for the loss of wheat and malt served to the court while in residence.

Just how efficacious the waters were is difficult to ascertain. Benjamin Allen, in the "Natural History of the Chalybeat Waters of England", published in 1699, described the water weighed at Red Well as "being eighteen grains lighter than common water". He added that a variety of colours were obtained when mixing with certain tinctures and syrups. Logwood and cloves produced black, violets a deep green, and galls violet. Exactly what benefits these additives achieved however is not recorded.

Despite extensive research for their comprehensive "History of Wellingborough" published in 1972, Joyce and Maurice Palmer were unable to unearth a single pictorial representation of the famous well, but we can be certain that an elaborate structure was once erected on the site. An entry in the Town Book for 1640 refers to the completion of timber and stonework repairs at a total cost of ten pounds two shillings, perhaps reflecting hopes that the Royal family might once more grace Wellingborough with their patronage.

Regrettably, Charles was then beset with problems of far greater import than the fostering of distant watering places, probably limiting his visits in those troubled times to more convenient wells at Tunbridge and Epsom. The Red Well never enjoyed such eminence again. Evidence of its decline can be found in Beeby Thompson's "Named Springs of Northamptonshire", which informs us that in 1797, on the site of the spring, stood

".... a large stone watering trough which was used by attendents upon horses ..... as a place at which to refresh their animals. It was sufficiently large to admit twenty horses to drink together. The water was made to pass through a sculptured head and came pouring out with considerable force at the mouth".

By 1823 a watermill, later known as Kilborn Mill, had been built not far from the site and at its opening, a poem by one Thomas Dexter was read to the large gathering. It contained

these verses,

"That well, which in days that are gone

Was held in such note and esteem

That Royalty stoop'd from her throne

To drink its salubrious stream.

But, alas, as the years rolled along

Forsaken was yon little spot!

No more the resort of the throng -

Neglected, despised and forgot".

The people of Wellingborough were to derive an unexpected benefit from the Spring Waters during the late nineteenth century. A pumping station was build adjacent to the mill, directing water to a reservoir, from where it flowed by gravitation to both the Woolston and Dulley breweries in Sheep Street. Here the water was used in the manufacture of

beer. A reminder of its origin was commemorated in one particular product, Redwell Stout, in which form the well water doubtless continued to do wonders for the "fissyness, sluggishness and restiness of the vessels." (Both breweries were later acquired by Campbell Praed and Co. whose premises once occupied a large site in the town centre).

In the eighteen sixties George de Wilde, then editor of the Northampton Mercury, spent his rare holidays exploring the Northamptonshire countryside. One such ramble roundabout led him in search of the historic well. He wrote,"A pleasant walk of about a mile along the Kettering Road, brings you to a mill on the left hand side of the way. Crossing the stile into the mill field, and following the winding stream which turns the wheel, to its source, you reach the once famous well - a site thoroughly secluded and very picturesque. The spring is strong. Scoop a handful and drink, and you recognise at once the flavour of the "flat irons" as immortal Sam Weller says".

I retraced De Wilde's steps one cold day last December. Kilborn Mill has long disappeared, but a road that bears its name borders the large open area above the Hatton Brook. Metalled paths criss cross, there are occasional oases of shrubs planted amongst the grass and ubiquitous signs warn off would be golfers.

Yet nothing indicates the whereabouts of the celebrated well. I found this difficult to believe and retracing my steps I consulted officials in the Council Offices in Swanspool. There I was provided with an explanation, a seasonal mince pie and large scale map. Thus equipped I returned to quickly locate two undistinguished grassy mounds, topped with iron drain covers, behind a row of prefabricated garages in Somerford Road.

As late as 1811 a letter to the Northampton Mercury outlined plans to build a pumproom and lay out grounds on the Redwell site in the style of Bath with a view to establishing Wellingborough as a Spa town.

Perhaps with kindness, and in the fullness of time, the new plantations will create a more hospitable setting than on that bleak winter morning. It was certainly difficult to visualise any elegant Georgian crescent, or to imagine a Royal Pavilion gracing the windswept turf.

Bath, Buxton, Tunbridge Wells, Leamington Spa. Failure to capitalise upon the Red Well's early promise of celebrity status destroyed any chance of adding Wellingborough to that impressive list. Today, despite local schools and a Leisure Centre bearing the famous name, the historic site itself is truly, "neglected, despised and forgot". Perhaps the spirit of awareness now alive in the town will one day generate a more fitting memorial.

13

"I SHALL NEVER CEASE TO LOVE HER DEAD"

In the summer of 1907 the people of St Albans staged a pageant re-enacting events from the city's illustrious past. Artist Frank Salisbury was so moved by one particular tableau that he resolved to record its pageantry on a huge canvas, all of fifteen feet long and five feet high. The result was a remarkable painting, vivid and compelling in Pre-Raphaelite style, entitled "The Passing of Queen Eleanor."

For many years the picture hung in the South Trancept of St Albans Abbey close to the very spot where the coffin of Edward I's Queen rested on its final journey from Lincoln Cathedral to Westminster Abbey in December 1290. It seemed a fitting replacement for the fine stone cross that had respectfully commemorated the tragic event before Cromwell's soldiers attacked the monument during the Civil War, council officials completing its demolition in 1801. Sadly, similar contempt for our historical heritage was repeated on the night of October 14th 1973. Thieves entered the Abbey through a vestry window, removed Salisbury's vast painting from its frame, rolled the altar silver, candlesticks and a splendid processional cross inside and made their escape. Some of the silver was eventually recovered but the painting has been consigned to oblivion.

Today's visitors must content themselves with a postcard sized version still available from the Cathedral shop. Which all serves to show that in Northamptonshire we are truly twice blessed, as the following story will hopefully reveal.

In late September 1290 Edward and Eleanor spent their last days together at Rockingham Castle in the heart of that vast Royal forest, which in those days covered most of middle England. They had then been happily married for over thirty years. No mean feat for a couple whose betrothal had been little more than an act of political expediency, part of a pact which ended war between England and Aquitaine in the middle of the 13th century. Edward, heir apparent to the English throne, was just fifteen. His bride, daughter of Ferdinand III of Castile and Leon in Northern Spain, was only nine.

It was ten years before they began married life together. Their mutual attraction demanded that Eleanor regularly accompanied her husband on military expeditions to far flung parts of the medieval world. During the fifth crusade to Jerusalem, begun in 1270, Eleanor is reputed to have saved Edward's life by sucking poison from a wound received from the dipped weapon of a Saracen. Edward was the last English Crusader. (Ironically it was to commemorate the entry into Jerusalem by General Allenby and the men of the Hertfordshire Regiment in 1917 that Frank Salisbury's painting was presented to St Albans Abbey by the Mayor, Alderman A Faulkner)

It was on this expedition that Edward learned of the death of his father, Henry III, and on their return to England in 1272 the couple were crowned King and Queen.

The marriage produced at least fifteen children of whom only one son survived. He (the ill-fated Edward II), was invested as the first Prince of Wales following his birth at Caernavon Castle in 1284.

The times were troubled. In an attempt to pacify rebellious elements in Scotland the infant Edward was betrothed to the heir of the Scottish throne, young Maid of Norway. Prospects for peace were dashed however when Maid died in 1290 throwing Scotland into turmoil once more.

Edward responded to news of the deteriorating situation by hastening north at the head of his army, his wife as usual at his side. At Rockingham further despatches convinced the King that he must proceed with greater urgency and so Eleanor was left behind. It would appear that his departure coincided with the onset of her illness. An extant bill dated only a few days later records that "apothecary stuff" was dispensed to the ailing queen to treat an "autumn fever." She followed Edward slowly northward but by the time she reached Grantham in mid-October her condition had worsened. She died at Harby in Nottinghamshire on the 28th November at the house of a "Gentleman named Richard Weston."

On receiving news of her critical condition Edward had quickly retraced his journey, but it is doubtful if he ever saw Eleanor alive again.

The Queen's body was first conveyed to Lincoln where, in common with medieval practice, the heart was removed and interred in the Cathedral. The journey of the funeral cortege to London, a distance of over 150 miles by the old routes, began on December 4th, reached Westminster almost a fortnight later and necessitated about a dozen overnight stops. The rough terrain would have required the coffin to be carried on a rudimentary cart for much of the journey. Yet in the postcard version, Frank Salisbury's painting clearly shows a wax effigy of the dead queen resting on a bier. This may be artistic licence but in the Cathedral Year book of 1959 Salisbury maintains that the wax effigy was used to provide models of the stone figure of Eleanor at Lincoln Cathedral and the full scale bronze casting in Westminster Abbey.

It appears likely therefore that the bier was specially prepared

"The coffin was carried on a rudimentary cart."

and decorated on entry to the more auspicious resting places such as St Albans.

Edward adopted the custom then common on the continent, and in fact employed to commemorate his uncle King Louis IX of France, of erecting a memorial cross to mark the place where the cortege rested, although his English stone monuments were far grander in design.

> 'Where'er the coffin bearers stayed
>
> Upon that long and tedious way
>
> A cross of stone King Edward made
>
> And some are standing to this day."

The first three, erected at Lincoln, Grantham and Stamford, have long since disappeared but the fourth remains, largely unaltered, in the small village of Geddington a few miles to the north east of Kettering.

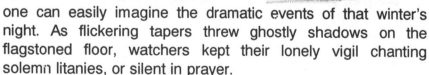

Overlooking the cross is the Parish Church of St Mary Magdalen where the body of Queen Eleanor rested seven hundred years ago.

Standing for a few moments in the nave of that fine church one can easily imagine the dramatic events of that winter's night. As flickering tapers threw ghostly shadows on the flagstoned floor, watchers kept their lonely vigil chanting solemn litanies, or silent in prayer.

Just a short distance away, where now stand bungalows and the aptly named Castle Garden flats, the King spent that same night in the Royal Hunting Lodge, one of his favourite places and a reminder of happier times. Originally erected in 1129 the building was regularly occupied by Royal parties hunting in Rockingham forest for the following 160 years. Henry II used the Lodge frequently, holding two Great Councils there. In 1194 Richard I entertained King William of Scotland and there are several records of visits by King John.

Geddington's is regarded as the finest of the three surviving memorial crosses. Completed between 1291 and 1294 it stands 12 metres high on a rising hexagonal plinth set on a mount now comprising seven stone steps. The triangular shaft is in three stages and full of interest, historical significance and fine workmanship.

The lowest stage is decorated with a myriad of flowers, leaves and geometric shapes all weathered and difficult to delineate. Six shields, two to each face, carry the armorial bearings of Castile and Leon, Ponthieu in France, and England. Oddly enough the coat of arms adopted by Eleanor's father Ferdinand and displayed on the cross utilised a design originally sketched by the famous medieval historian and chronicler Matthew Paris, a Benedictine monk from, of all places, St Alban's Abbey.

The middle storey features three differing studies of the Queen in the form of stone figures, each standing in canopied niches. Although commonly described as "weeping queens" the veiled figures merely display the accustomed travelling attire favoured by ladies in the thirteenth century and should not necessarily imply mourning.

The third stage is hexagonal with pinnacles crowned with small gables ornamented with oak leaves and surmounted with fleurs-de-lys. It is possible that the whole structure was once further adorned by a cross.

On sunny afternoons, swathed in sunlight, the monument

affects a timeless, serene quality at the heart of a peaceful English village. At night, however, floodlit against a darkened backdrop of cottage, church and sky, it assumes a more melancholy aspect. The duality of Man's nature appears embodied in Edward's tribute to his beloved Queen. For this was also the king who massacred Jews in Northampton, ruthlessly suppressed Scottish dissidents and subjected Llewellyn, Wales' legitimate Prince, to barbaric humiliation and death.

The cortege next rested nineteen miles away at the Cluniac nunnery at De-La-Pre, built by Simon de Senlis, Earl of Northampton in the twelfth century. The cross was built between 1291 and 1293 alongside the Northampton to Stony Stratford road at Hardingstone on the outskirts of Delapre Park.

Naturally there are similarities with the Geddington memorial, but as all twelve crosses were believed to have been unique, it is not surprising to note significant differences.

An octagonal shaft is set on a mount of nine steps. The lowest stage had buttresses at the angles, its faces flat and adorned with shields bearing Royal Arms shown hanging and wreathed. Four of the faces have carvings of open books set on lecterns. The second storey contains four statues of Eleanor, this time unveiled, facing the points of the compass. One figure is depicted surcoted while the other three are mantled. Above, the third stage rises from a series of gables and spires. This tapering, four faced, buttressed structure supports the broken shaft of the cross, damaged centuries ago. Indeed as early as 1460 John Stone, an eyewitness at the Battle of Northampton, records observing the carnage "from a hille called Headless Cross."

In subsequent years pilgrims retracing Eleanor's final journey travelled from Northampton's South Bridge to the memorial by a paved causeway, referred to in a 1586 survey as "Rotten Row or Row of the Rood Cross."

A copy of the foot and first stage of the cross is incorporated in the font in Northampton's St Peter's Church, dating from about 1320.

From Hardingstone the funeral procession continued its journey southward to Westminster and crosses were duly erected at Stony Stratford, Woburn, Dunstable, St Alban's, Waltham, West Cheap and Charing. It is likely that all these other memorials, save that at Waltham, met a similar fate to St Albans' and were destroyed during the Civil War. The original cross at Charing, said to derive from Cher Reine (dear Queen), was demolished in 1647. This act drew the following satirical response from a public rapidly tiring of such Parliamentary excesses.

> "... then fare thee well, old Charing Cross
>
> Fare thee well old stump.
>
> Thou was a thing set up by a King
>
> And so pulled down by the Rump ....."

The cross presently gracing the yard facing Charing Cross Station was erected in 1865 and is believed to be an accurate copy of the original. Its architect was E.M. Barry, son of the designer of the Houses of Parliament.

Edward was remarried nine years after his first wife's death, to Margaret, daughter of Philip II of France. However, words attributed to the King clearly demonstrate his affection for Eleanor,

> "Living I loved her tenderly,
>
> And I shall never cease to love her dead."

A love enshrined so enduringly in Northamptonshire's fine stone crosses.

14

MOMENTS OF THE ROSE

On the brow of a hill, silhouetted against an autumnal sky, stands a forlorn figure. It is a faithful copy of a fine statue, the Apollo Belvedere no less and rests on its plinth protected by a wooden fence and the shrivelled remains of the summer's sweetcorn crop. In such an isolated and forbidding spot one could suppose it to be no more than an elegant scarecrow.

But return to the track at the bottom of the slope, look across the overgrown ditch and you'll notice a carefully fashioned stone wall with parapet and low decorative iron fence. Beyond, amongst clumps of ubiquitous fir trees tower the occasional ancient cedar, yew and oak. And at your feet, suddenly, amongst years of untrodden leaf-fall is a tiny grey headstone. A memorial to Jack, died 1902, aged 9 years. A loved pet buried as we might today in a quiet corner of the garden. For garden this was. Exquisitely landscaped, cultivated with fine lawns and fountains, with servants employed to continuously weed its acres of gravel paths. The garden of a great house. Blatherwycke Hall.

Although its huge ornamental lake survives, at sixty acres the largest in Northamptonshire, you'll look in vain for remains of the splendid mansion. Amongst tangled undergrowth and gloomy firs, pheasant and rabbit now inhabit its ghostly corridors and stately rooms. Only the handsome stable block and its crumbling outbuildings still exist where tractor and farm machinery have supplanted the gig, and landau.

However, the adjacent church of the Holy Trinity, now administered by the Redundant Churches Commission from their splendidly named St Andrews-by-the-Wardrobe head-quarters, contains ample evidence of past glories.

Having acquired the key from a farmhouse in the village and entered the building in the gathering dusk of a late November afternoon, the atmosphere of this place is almost overwhelming, the past palpable, the ghosts undoubtedly watching.

> "..... while the light fails
>
> On a winter's afternoon, in a secluded chapel
>
> History is now and England".

For history, dusty and grime encrusted, fills every corner. Sturdy Norman pillars, Tudor monuments, box pews, a beautifully carved wooden Jacobean pulpit and canopy, and impressive Victorian stained glass.

Yet it is the abundance of memorials that provides the strongest link with the past. A splendid brass, alongside an ornate stone monument, supported by Ionic pillars with carved figures in relief, depict Tudor Staffords, one of whom, Sir Humphrey, built the original Blatherwycke Hall. He then, rather surprisingly, began work in 1570 on another even more splendid house just a few miles away. Kirby Hall. On his death the property was acquired by Sir Christopher Hatton who completed the project. In 1640 the more famous Hatton's descendent and namesake had erected a finely carved marble tablet in the church, (created by Nicholas Stone, sculptor to the Royal household, at a cost of £10), in memory of a Thomas Randolph.

A remarkable man of sensitivity and talent, Randolph was born at Newnham near Daventry in 1605. After a brilliant career at Trinity College Cambridge, where he wrote several plays including his most renowned "The Muses Looking Glass", he moved to London and became a member of Ben Jonson's literary set. Regarded as 'among the most pregnant wits of his age' and a possible successor to Shakespeare, he never alas fulfilled his early promise. A licentious life style in the capital contributed to his ill health and necessitated his departure to the fresher air of the Northamptonshire countryside. He acquired the position of tutor to John Stafford's children. That he belatedly relished the simple delights of rural life is reflected in an ode to his pupil Master Anthony Stafford

> *"Come spur away!*
>
> *I have no patience for a longer stay*
>
> *But I must go down*
>
> *And leave the chargeable noise of this grand town.*
>
> *I will the country see:*
>
> *Where old simplicity*
>
> *Though hid in grey*
>
> *Doth look more gay*
>
> *Than foppery in plush and scarlet clad ..."*

Sadly he died at Blathwycke, reportedly from smallpox, at the age of 29.

The lines carved on Randolph's memorial tablet are attributed to Peter Hausted, who continues the county connection being the Oundle born playwright and protege of Christopher Hatton. (Incidently he later became vicar of Gretton and Rector of Old before serving as Chaplain to Spencer, Earl of Northampton, at the beginning of the Civil War. He died in 1645 during the siege of Banbury Castle).

His words echo the metaphysical style of his fellow poet.

> *"Here sleep thirteen together in one tomb*
>
> *And all these great, yet quarrel not for room ..."*

It is a tribute to Thomas Randolph that despite a brief life and relatively sparse output the tattered visitor's book records a "pilgrimage to his final resting place" by an admirer from Houston in Texas.

More light-heartedly, another tablet commemorates two bene-factors to the poor of Blatherwycke parish. Thomas Cole's bequest is decidedly unusual. His will required that from his death in 1684, profits from the sale of wood coppiced in a close on his land in nearby Kingscliffe, should provide forever "six of the oldest poor men in the parish a plum pudding on Christmas Day".

In the Christmas Eve edition of the Evening Telegraph" in 1974 the Rev Lloyd Caddick, then rector of Holy Trinity Church and a trustee of the Coles estate, commented on the current state of the legacy.

"I don't know when the plum puddings were last distributed but I believe it was within living memory. I should imagine that rent from the land which is let will be distributed to the six oldest and poorest men in the parish, but how does one decide who they are?"

Benjamin Healy left a more conventional legacy. The interest of one hundred pounds deposited in the O'Briens hands for the use of the poor. Who you may well ask were the O'Briens?

They were supposedly descended from Brian Bora, King of Ireland in 1002, and were united with the Staffords by marriage in 1699. (The Stafford love knot is carved on several houses in the village, while the arm and dagger symbol of the O'Briens defiantly appears on the stable block beneath the monogram of one Donatus, dated 1770).

The Elizabethan house was replaced in 1723 by a large and handsome Georgian building, surrounded by a deerpark of 400 acres, "on an eminence which afforded extensive views".

Designed by Thomas Ripley and built by local man Robert Wright, it was home to the successive generations of Stafford O'Briens, whose remains now lie in the family vault.

The family, however, traditionally low Anglicans, were not always in harmony with the established church. The Hon. E. O'Brien, a man born well before his time, published a pamphlet in 1838 urging greater understanding between Protestants and Catholics. Eight years later Sir Henry Dryden, an antiquarian and archaelogist wrote of Blatherwycke,

'It is the seat of the O'Briens who keep a grand house and a church which would disgrace the poorest villager".

This comment may reflect the effects of a dispute between patron and cleric when the rector made known his intention for the church to become "high". A ruined Gothic window at the back of the stable block, overlooking an overgrown corner of the churchyard, indicates where alternative services may have been held during the feud.

Another small mystery involves the Norman style font which bears an intriguing dedication on its base.

"In memory of a merciful deliverance

from drowning in the river Nith September 12th 1840".

A Stafford O'Brien.

Intriguing, because I assume the incident is linked in many publications to a back to front gravestone outside in the churchyard, whose inscription reads:

In memory of

Anthony Williams

who was drowned

(in Blatherwycke Lake)

June 11th 1836

Aged 29 years.

"Here a poor wanderer hath found a grave

who death embraced when struggling with the wave".

Whether Anthony Williams, a black servant at the Hall, saved his master and perished in the act or coincidentally drowned in a later tragedy is a matter for conjecture.

Lucy Adele Lock in "Memories of a Villager" (1958) recalls a black statue, long disappeared, by the lake commemorating the rescue. In her account, however, the "boy" survived but died some years later, unable to withstand the cold English winters.

Presumably the same A. (Augustus Stafford O'Brien), the M.P. for North Northants, died in mysterious circumstances in Dublin in 1857.

Back in the church a grimy memorial brass tells us that during the Crimean War he had visited the field hospital at Scutari where his compassion for the wounded and dying soldiers in their "tents and infected holds of transports" won much admiration. (While his near neighbour at Deene Hall, the Earl of Cardigan, achieved notoriety in that campaign by leading the ill fated Charge of the Light Brigade).

Augustus endured recurring respiratory problems resulting from privations suffered in the Crimea which probably contributed to his early death. The death certificate registered "heart disease", but observers at the time hinted at an overdose of laudanum, much used at the time to alleviate pain, administered by a careless physician.

His epitaph reads:

> *"Beloved till life can charm no more*
>
> *And mourned till memories*
>
> *self be dead".*

Throughout the nineteenth century Blatherwycke Hall continued to reflect the grandeur of the family, many of whom like Augustus' successor Henry who became High Sheriff for the County in 1868, achieved distinction in public life. It retained a huge complement of servants, coaches rolled up to the elegant portico and its stables were filled with hunters on which the family and guests rode to hounds. But this golden age was not destined to survive long into the new century.

The loss of their huge 25,000 acre Irish estates, during land nationalisation following independence in 1921, crippled the family financially. They could not afford to repair the inestimable damage to the Hall wreaked by troops billeted there during the second world war. They had little option but to sell for a few thousand pounds. Its value as building materials.

In September 1948 the two surviving Stafford O'Briens at

Blatherwycke, Miss Matilda Finola and Miss Lucy Mary watched the demolition of their stately home. There were mixed feelings, for in the "Kettering Leader" Tony Ireson recalls how the two sisters were happy to be re-housed in a "wooden bungalow built in the sunny high walled orchard and kitchen garden .... delightfully kept under the shadow of the ancient church".

However they must have deplored the wanton destruction of the once great house.

Ireson describes the decay and ruination. "Windows are broken, there are gaping holes in the roof where slates are missing, plaster has tumbled from walls and gilt ornamentation fallen from cornices". Yet glimpses of departed glories remained, amongst them marble statues of two women in Grecian style, brought from abroad. Part of a batch perhaps that included the Apollo Belvedere?

The demolition men and their bulldozers did the work well. Everything was removed or salvaged and today, search as you will, nothing remains to show where the mansion once stood.

Sections of ornamental iron fence lie toppled at the edge of the churchyard. only the gateway leading from the hall remains, ironically locked. Barring the way from nowhere to a redundant church, whose tower contains the mechanism of the clock that once graced the stable block and whose interior houses as we have seen many silent testaments to former greatness. Its face overlooks the neglected graveyard, where its donor, Miss Matilda lies buried alongside her sister. A short distance away Jack, their pet dog, still sleeps beneath the leaf litter.

But as T.S. Eliot reflected:

> *"The moment of the rose*
> *and the moment of the yew tree*
> *are of equal duration"*

And on the brow of the hill, moved there by thoughtful workmen in deference to his former station among the neo-classical splendours of a grand house and its fine lawns, the lonely sentinel keeps his silent vigil.

BIBLIOGRAPHY

A History of Northamptonshire, R L Greenhall, (1979)

Transactions of the Royal Historical Society

The Raunds Strike and March to London 1905, J R Betts, (1989)

An Epic Example of Trade Unionism, Allen and Bartley, (1934)

James Gribble and the Raunds Strike of 1905, Keith Brooker, (Northants Past and Present)

Charles Wicksteed, Hilda Wicksteed, (Dent, 1933)

Jerry and Grandpa, Hilda Wicksteed, (Harrap, 1930)

Kettering Revisited, Tony Smith, (Wharton, 1993)

Finedon otherwise Thingdon, John L H Bailey, (1975)

A History of Fotheringhay, S J Hunt, (1987)

Some Ancient Interests of Fotheringhay, R A Muntz

I Saw Two Englands, H V Morton, (Methuen, 1942)

Northamptonshire, T Ireson, (R Hale, 1954)

The Tragedy of Fotheringhay, Mrs Maxwell Scott, (1924)

Gervase Elwes, Winifrede R Elwes, (Grayson & Grayson, 1935)

Great Billing Hall and the Elwes Family, Jerome Betts, (Northants Local History News, 1994)

A Right To Song, Edward Storey, (Methuen, 1982)

The Life of John Clare, Frederick Martin, (Macmillan, 1865)

Aviation in Northamptonshire, Michael Gibson, (Northants Libraries, 1982)

The Elephant Man and Other Reminisences, Sir Frederick Treves, (1923)

The Illustrated True History of the Elephant Man, Howell & Ford, (Penguin, 1983)

Portrait of Northamptonshire, P G Webb, (R Hale, 1977)

Northamptonshire, A Mee, (Hodder & Stoughton, 1945)

Northamptonshire Landscape, J M Steane, (Hodder & Stoughton, 1974)

F A Book For Boys 1953-54

H E Bates - A Literary Life, Dean Baldwin, (Ass Univ Press USA, 1987)

H E Bates - A Bibliographical Study, P Eads, (St Paul, 1990)

Give Them Their Life - The Poetry of H E Bates, P Eads, (London, 1990)

The Book of Leisure, J Pudney, (Odhams, 1957)

The Vanished World, H E Bates, (Michael Joseph, 1969)

The Blossoming World, H E Bates, (Michael Joseph, 1971)

Rambles Roundabout, George de Wilde, (Edit E Dicey, 1872)

Railway World, Ian Allan, (1977)

The De Wildes, Ian Mayes & Northampton Museum, (1971)

Queen Eleanor and her Crosses, Joyce Palmer, (Northants & Beds Life)

St Albans Cathedral Year Book and Electoral Roll, (1959)

Geddington As It Was, Monica Rayne, (1991)

A History Of Wellingborough, J & M Palmer, (Steepleprint, 1972)

History of Wellingborough, John Cole, (Daly, 1837)

Peculiarities of Waters and Wells, Beeby Thompson, (Northants Natural History Society)

Sketches in Prose and Verse, John Askham, (1893)

Poems and Sonnets, John Askham, (1866)

Now and Then - the life and times of Bulwick etc Vol 2, Bob Howe

Blatherwycke Village Memoirs, Lucy A Lock

Northamptonshire in the 20th Century - Contemporary Biographies, W T Pike

Squires Homes and other old buildings of Northamptonshire, J A Gotch

The Nude, Kenneth Clark, (J Murray, 1956)

A Northamptonshire Garland, Trevor Hold, (Northants Library, 1989)

Natural History of Northamptonshire, John Morton, (1712)

Northamptonshire Curiosities, Chris Billing, (Dovecote Press, 1993)

Exploring Northamptonshire, Tony Noble, (Meridian Books, 1987)

The Kettering Reminder, Kettering Public Library

Royal Northamptonshire, Northamptonshire Libraries

Drawing of Billing Hall after Frederick W Payne